EARTH KNACK

BART AND ROBIN BLANKENSHIP own and operate Earth Knack, a school that teaches Stone Age living skills. Weekend seminars and one- to three-week courses include all the subjects in this book as well as many others, such as bow and arrow, felting, atlatl, fiber sandals, edibles and medicinals, and numerous ways of incorporating these skills into modern lifestyles. If you'd like to know more, contact Bart and Robin at the following address:

Earth Knack
P.O. Box 19693
Boulder, CO 80308

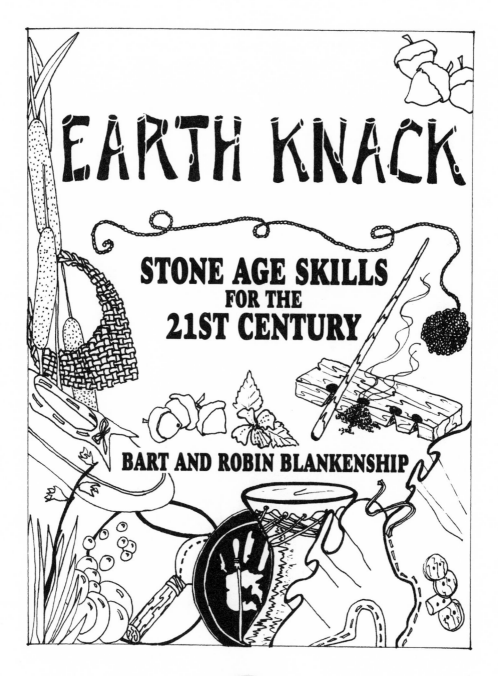

EARTH KNACK

STONE AGE SKILLS
FOR THE
21ST CENTURY

BART AND ROBIN BLANKENSHIP

GIBBS·SMITH
P
PUBLISHER

SALT LAKE CITY

First edition
99 98 97 96 8 7 6 5 4 3 2 1

This is a Peregrine Smith Book, published by
Gibbs Smith, Publisher
P.O. Box 667
Layton, Utah 84041

Design by J. Scott Knudsen, Park City, Utah
Cover photographs by David Patryas, Boulder,
Colorado, © 1996 by Gibbs Smith, Publisher
Printed and bound in the United States of America

Library of Congress Cataloging-in-Publication Data

Blankenship, Bart, 1958-
Earth Knack: stone age skills for the 21st century / Bart
and Robin Blankenship. —1st ed.
p.   cm.
ISBN 0-87905-733-5
1. Handicraft. 2. Nature craft. I. Blankenship, Robin,
1959- . II. Title.
TT157.B615 1996
745.5—dc20
                        95-43690
                        CIP

CONTENTS

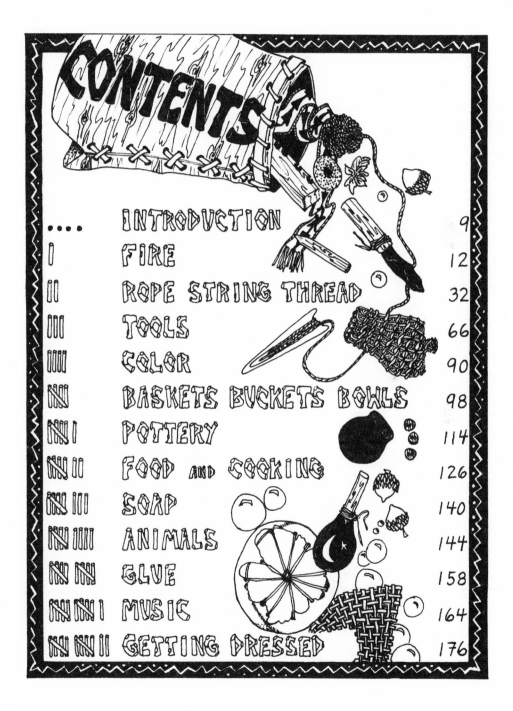

INTRODUCTION

EARTH KNACK
A daily living skills guide using Stone Age techniques for finding and making what you need in your local environment.

FEW OF US ARE REALLY GOING TO "CHUCK IT ALL" and live as hunter-gatherers in the wilds, like our Stone Age ancestors did. Yet, becoming a modern hunter-gatherer, developing a knack for living with the Earth in any enviornment, is well within our grasp. Using age-old skills, which are still perfectly applicable to our modern lifestyles, can enrich our daily lives and bring high levels of satisfaction and fullfillment.

This book is a comprehensive guide to gathering and creating many things to fulfill your daily needs from materials readily at hand. As you assimilate this knowledge into your daily life, you will find the variety of things you can do and make to be endless. You will be able to replace many modern purchased items and foodstuffs with things you gather and create from your local environment. You will also find these Stone Age skills environmentally appropriate and uniquely fulfilling. Besides all this, being paleolithically proficient is a lot of fun!

Developing a knack for living with the Earth is not that difficult, and many people are intrigued by the thought of learning and using Stone Age living skills in their modern lives. Yet it seems the first question most would-be paleos ask themselves is, "How much time do these skills take?" Living in the modern era means our day is dictated by time. Time has, in fact, become our most precious commodity, our most valued resource. Finding, gathering, and making what we need does take time, yet some skills are surprisingly time-efficient.

To address this issue we have chosen projects and techniques where the outcome is more than worth the investment of your time. This is what we call *return*. Before each new endeavor we ask ourselves, "What is the return?

Is this a project worth undertaking? Will my time and energy be rewarded?" For the items in this book, the answer is "Yes!" for a variety of reasons. For example, here are just a few projects and activities that have a high return:

- It takes only one blow with a hammer stone on a piece of rock to yield a sharp cutting edge.
- It takes an hour to gather several pounds of acorns.
- Collecting needles for pine needle tea, extremely high in vitamins B and C, is easy.
- The soapwort plant grows everywhere in our area. Just add water and rub and your reward will be a rich soapy lather.
- Hide glue is one of the strongest glues known and is completely natural.

Of course, there is more to return than just the end result. The process provides return as well. As you explore your environment while gathering materials and foods, a world of lost knowledge opens up to you. Materials, once unknown and therefore unseen, become apparent. As you plan your project or prepare a new food, you find an outlet for creativity. When you use your clay cooking pot, wear your buckskin shirt, or serve steaming hot acorn muffins with chokecherry jelly, you experience a level of satisfaction hard to beat. From the initial gathering and preparation to using the finished product, you experience good return for your time and energy.

There are many other reasons for reaching back to the quickly disappearing skills and arts of the Stone Age. There is a great sense of fulfillment in knowing and using materials in your area to meet your daily needs. Being able to make what you need allows you to choose what you want. No longer are you limited to what's on the store shelf. And being part of the decision, design, and development of your daily needs allows you to bypass the apathy that often follows a new purchase and all too quickly leaves you thinking only about what to buy next. You become part of the process and experience fulfillment along the way *as well as* pride in the use or consumption of the final product.

We all want to feel capable. Learning and using the Stone Age skills builds self-reliance. Self-esteem increases as you learn to create a comfortable lifestyle. Food, clothing, containers, soap, glue, vitamins, fire, and light become things you can make for yourself. These skills are empowering. Now that's "return"!

Let's look at the environment. All sides of the political spectrum are talking about it. We are all familiar with the current slogan "Reduce, Reuse, Recycle." Incorporating Stone Age skills into our daily lives provides an opportunity to be an example of a conscious and workable environmental philosophy. We become very conscious of the precious resources growing all around us, and we suddenly have a vested interest in keeping them in *good* condition. That field has our dinner, that hillside our clothing, that gully our tools! This is bioregionalism at its best. We become part and parcel of our environmental community.

Social community takes on a whole new relevance. Each of us has a heritage in the Stone Age no matter what culture we come from, what religion we profess, or what nationality we pledge allegiance to. In a world that divides us in so many ways, here is one common base, a valid basis to build a foundation of community.

Many people today are seeking a stronger spiritual connection and delving into the past for answers. Celtic ritual, Native American ceremony, and Goddess rites are all being probed, studied, and imitated. Stone Age skills were the foundation of the ceremonies, rites, and rituals. We put the cart before the horse when we practice the ancient rituals without first learning the skills from which these rituals sprang. And once you start living some of these ancient skills, you'll find you have an inherent, personal knowledge of your spiritual connection to the world.

Finally, the greatest motivation of all for incorporating Stone Age skills into your modern lifestyle: FUN! These skills are a real kick in the pants! When you create a fire for the first time by rubbing two pieces of wood together, the spark is in your eye as well as in the burning ember. Walking into your local movie theater dressed head to toe in buckskin you have tanned yourself is a thrill not to be missed. Hanging from the loaded branches of an apple tree growing in the median on Main Street will turn a lot of motorists' heads. You'll get to know your neighbors as you knock on doors asking to glean grapes, pick pears, or dig dock root. As you dig clay, grind acorns, make hand-drill fires, and roam your area looking for raw materials and edibles, you'll be adopting a personalized paleolithic fitness program. Then you will really have fun saving all that money that used to go the gym.

So go ahead and get the knack! Roll up your sleeves and put a grin on your face. A healthy and friendly world awaits the modern hunter-gatherer.

CHAPTER

I

FIRE

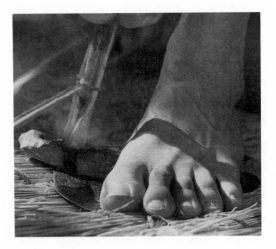

THERE IS MAGIC IN CREATING FIRE. Imagine focusing your energy enough to make something burn! The results of this effort are inspiring: the warmth of the fire, renewed feelings of capability, and pure delight. By performing a task that your ancestors did daily—the simple movements, the honest effort—you also earn passage into that déjà vu of a million years, that connection in genetic memory to ages past. Creating fire is a powerful experience.

Fire may seem obsolete in our modern, urban lifestyles. After all, we have the thermostat, the oven, the electric blanket, the dishwasher, the hot water tank. But don't fool yourself. No matter how we change the packaging—from electricity to propane, from coal to the Porsche pancake engine, from a diesel generator to nuclear fusion—we are still a fire-based culture. There is that spark behind almost everything we do.

There are many great projects and ideas in this book to enrich your modern lifestyle and broaden your possibilities on many fronts. Some of the ideas can change your life. But none of the projects is quite as ground-shaking as creating a friction fire! So pocket that Bic and give it a try. If nothing else, it's a tremendous icebreaker at your next party or a real showstopper when you go to light the Saturday barbecue.

GETTING READY

Three ways of making a friction fire are described in this chapter. In each method, you use a friction-fire set to create a small powdery ember called a "coal." The friction of the pieces of wood on each other creates a dust pile,

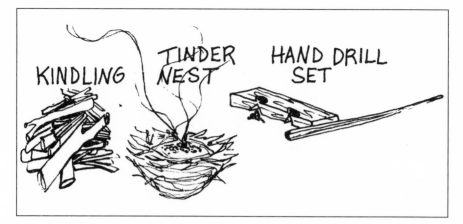

and the heat from the friction ignites the dust to form the coal. This coal is then placed in a nest of tinder and blown to a flame.

Whatever way you choose to make your friction fire, you will need tinder and kindling.

So gather your tinder and kindling first. Preparing tinder is the same for each of the three fire methods described in this chapter. Prepare the tinder and make a tinder nest before you start rubbing sticks to form the coal.

Here's how to make the tinder nest: You can use dry grass, fuzzed-up bark such as juniper, sage, and cliff rose; inner bark of aspen and cottonwood; or, in a pinch, tiny wood shavings. Generally, you want to fuzz up the tinder so it will catch fire easily. You want it to be soft and pliable. When you fuzz it, little bits will fall down from your hands as fine dust. You will need to save this dust, so work over a bandanna or something similar.

The best way we have found to work the tinder is to grab a length of it in both hands and move your fists round and round like they were pedaling a bike. This will soften the tinder that is between your hands. Move up and down the full length of your tinder. Then take some of this prepared tinder and tie a loose overhand knot in it. The diameter of the knot should be about four inches. Then stuff some tinder in this knot to make it like a bird's nest. Keep stuffing the nest until it is dense. You don't want the coal to fall through the fibers and out of the nest.

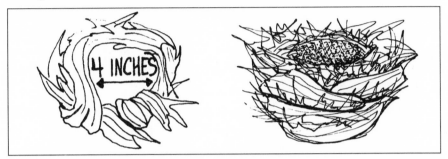

Make a small depression in the center of the nest to hold the dust that has fallen into your bandanna. As you pick up the dust you will notice that the finest particles fall back down onto the bandanna. This is what you want because you'll be packing finer and finer dust into the depression until the finest dust will be on the top, just where you'll place the eventual coal. Now make a small indentation in this dust for the coal and set the nest out of the way where the wind won't blow it and it won't get knocked.

One more thing before you start: check your kindling pile and make sure you have enough wood to get the fire established once you have a flame. That tinder nest won't burn forever, you know, and in the euphoria that comes once that tinder nest starts blazing, it's hard to make yourself jump up and dash around looking for scattered kindling.

In explaining these three friction fire methods, we give some specific dimensions to make your experience more successful. These are not hard and fast rules. After all, this isn't nuclear fusion, just the predecessor to it. Use the dimensions as guidelines.

FIRE-PLOW METHOD

Let's start out by getting really primitive! The first method is the **fire plow,** or literally rubbing two sticks together. It doesn't get any more basic

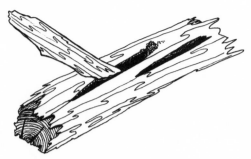

than this unless you're chasing lightning around!

Three-hundred-pound Polynesians have contests doing the fire plow. You don't *have* to be a sumo wrestler to do it, but this method does take intense effort. The first time we ever got this simple fire-starting method to work, we had twenty third graders and six adults to provide the muscle. Since then we have refined our techniques so that we can get it with just two or three of us, even in damp weather, and solo if conditions are bone dry. The beauty of it is that you don't need *any* tools to carve the wood. If you can break off a branch or a large splinter of wood and rub it against a log, you can be sitting around a warm fire while others are still whittling their more advanced fire sets.

The fire plow lets you get your weight right over the area you are working and uses large muscle groups that were made for power. Its drawback is that the heat is dispersed along a groove and it usually takes all that power to get a fire. Still, this is a time-tested method as well as a great workout.

Our favorite woods for this method are cottonwood and sotol (a type of *big* yucca). Both of these woods work well.

To make the plow, take a stick that is a foot long and comes to a point. Make the first inch of the smallest end of the stick between 1/4 and 1/2 inch wide. Your stick might already be this wide; if not, you can make the point like this with a knife or by rubbing it against a rough rock. The narrower the tip the more concentrated the heat, but the deeper it will dig into the log, or base. And the deeper the plow digs into the base, the harder it will be to push back and forth quickly to get a coal.

1 FOOT LONG

1" WIDE →

½" TO ¼" WIDE

Now use the plow to make a groove in the base log of the fire-plow set. (The base need not be large; it just has to be at least two inches wide.) Start off with the plow stick at right angles with the base. Push back and forth to indent a groove about six inches long. If the base is a stick and not a log, you may have to flatten the base or indent this groove first with a knife to keep the plow from slipping out. If it is a big log, just start plowing slowly. Have one hand an inch from the tip of the plow and the other with the palm over the butt end.

Once the groove is made, you're ready to get to work. Lower the butt end of the plow so that the contact area between the plow and the base is greater. The friction will dry out the wood and build up heat without gouging too deeply into the base.

PLOW AT RIGHT ANGLE TO BASE

INDENTING THE GROOVE

6" LONG

Once the wood is really smoking and black dust is forming, raise the butt end of the plow to focus the heat on the tip. Keep plowing back and forth, touching the accumulating dust at the far end of the groove every other time or so without obliterating this dust pile. Getting this subtle "touch and retreat" technique takes practice. Keep at it! You'll get the rhythm.

As you work the plow back and forth, sometimes a lip will form in the groove just before the place where the dust pile is accumulating. Each time you hit this lip, you can be snuffing out a potential coal with the plow. Hitting the lip also hinders your momentum and decreases dust accumulation. If a lip forms in the groove, either move the stroke of the plow forward a little to break through the lip, or move the stroke back so you don't touch it at all.

Speed and pressure are both important. If you find the accumulating dust is big and flaky, or if the plow is deepening the groove too quickly, use more speed and less pressure, or drop the butt end of the plow down to increase the contact area between the plow tip and the groove. This will harden the groove some so that it will wear more slowly and get sufficiently hot without wearing too deeply. On the other hand, if you don't apply enough downward pressure, a shiny black glaze will form, impeding friction. Your plow will slide easily in the base groove, but there won't be any smoke. Stop and clean the glaze off the plow stick and out of the base groove with a rough rock, or put sand in the groove and plow through the glaze.

If the groove gets so deep that it is hard to move the plow, sometimes you can shift your pressure forty-five degrees out to the side of the groove. This widens the groove instead of continuing to make it deeper. You can still get a coal this way without having to start a new groove.

You will find that as you plow and work at touching and retreating from the forming dust pile, the groove will shorten and you will be primarily using the half of the groove closest to you. If you allow the groove to get too short, you will be spending all your time plowing tiny strokes back and forth and you won't be able to get enough speed. Keep the groove at least three inches long even if you have to extend the groove toward you as you plow.

The fire plow method is a sprint. If you start to slow down, then switch and let someone else go at it. While you're switching, always keep the tip of the plow buried in the dust so you don't lose heat.

Once you get a coal with your fire-plow set, transfer it to your tinder bundle and blow it to a flame. Do this carefully enough to keep the coal intact. Fold the nest around the coal to keep the coal from falling out, and lift the tinder to mouth level, inverting the nest somewhat. This inversion allows the heat from the coal to rise into the dense mass of the tinder nest.

Blow gently on the coal, allowing it to consume the dust. As you blow, keep pinching the nest around the coal just enough to keep the coal in the nest while you tip the nest over and blow up into it. Don't pinch so hard that you put the coal out! As you're blowing, if sparks are flying all over, pinch up the nest to surround and contain the burning tinder. If you don't close up the nest at this point, the burning tinder may fall out of the nest.

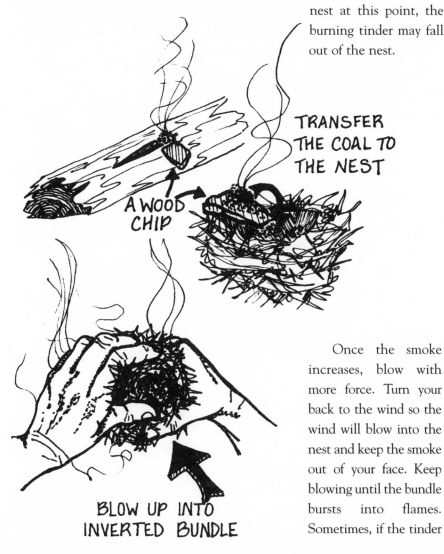

TRANSFER
THE COAL TO
THE NEST

A WOOD
CHIP

BLOW UP INTO
INVERTED BUNDLE

Once the smoke increases, blow with more force. Turn your back to the wind so the wind will blow into the nest and keep the smoke out of your face. Keep blowing until the bundle bursts into flames. Sometimes, if the tinder is damp, it may have to dry out before it can flame. So hold off blowing a minute to let the tinder dry out; then resume blowing. If the nest is too small or not dense enough and falling apart, you may need to add more dry material around the smoldering nest.

If your fingers get too hot, shift over to grabbing the nest between two sticks. A tough piece of folded bark with the nest jammed into the fold is another good way to hold it. The burning tinder soon becomes a roaring fire. That is, if you collected that kindling!

HAND-DRILL METHOD

Now we jump a million years or so in the evolution of fire making and do the **hand-drill** method. It involves rotating the flattened bottom of a stick very rapidly against a wooden base to create dust and a coal from the friction of the two woods.

This method ideally uses materials that are easy to fashion with crude tools. For example, the drill is usually a straight, slender stalk, 3/4 to 3/8 inch

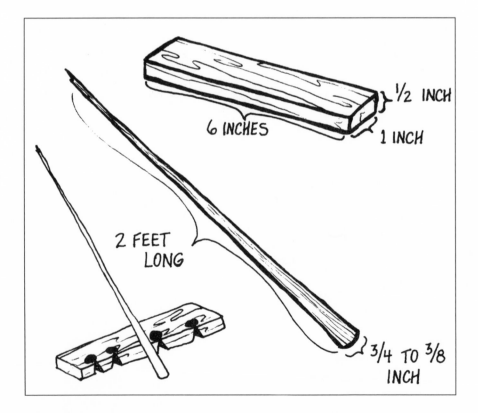

in diameter and a couple of feet long. It is no problem to cut down and smooth the stick with a knife or a sharp rock. The base against which the drill will be rotated needs to be about 1 inch wide, 1/2 inch thick, and 6 inches long. Sometimes, breaking off a dry branch will cause it to split, giving you a flat surface for your drill to spin against. So, this fire set is quick and easy to construct. It's also a good method for team fire making, since it is easy for folks to take turns spinning the drill.

A word of caution before you begin: most people's hands are soft. When you start practicing this method, especially if you are by yourself, don't get carried away and ignore the blisters forming on your palms, even if you are about to get a fire. Stop when it hurts. Wait a day or so and allow the skin on your hands to gradually toughen. Practice a little each day till your hands are ready. Also, the joints where your fingers join your palms may be sore the first few times after you do this. If you get big blisters and then big callouses (such as we have sometimes from doing what we just told you not to do), then these raised callouses will contact the drill with more force than the rest of your hand and you wind up with blisters under the calluses in a never-ending cycle.

Let's get the hand-drill set made. Woods that have worked for us for the hand-drill bases have been cottonwood, willow, alder, sage, yucca, incense cedar, juniper, and clematis. For the drills we have used yucca, cattail, seep willow, elderberry, and mullein. Experiment. You're sure to find plenty of other options.

You need to establish a hole in the base, then carve a notch to catch the coal dust. First, smooth out the drill so it won't chew up your hands. Then split the base wood flat like a board and make it wider than the drill and half an inch thick. Gouge out an indenta-

GOUGE AN INDENTATION SO ITS EDGE IS 1/8" FROM EDGE OF BASE-BOARD

tion in the base wood where you will spin the drill. This gouge should be no more than 1/8 inch from one edge of the base-board.

Hold the baseboard in place, either with your foot or by placing something heavy on it. Slightly wet your palms and put the drill in the gouge. Then rapidly spin the drill between your palms, applying lots of downward pressure. This is exactly how you'll work to make a coal, but this first step is for getting a hole for the drill to spin in and a notch in that hole to collect the coal dust. Make sure both hands are moving equally to keep the drill spinning without wobble. Drill down until the depression is about 1/16 inch deep, established enough to hold the drill without it sliding out and popping off the base when you start drilling to get the coal. The hole will be rounded and brown.

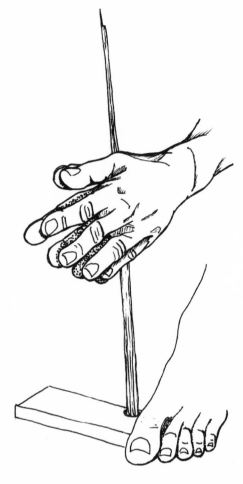

Once the hole is established, carve the notch in the hole with a sharp stone or a knife. The notch is important. A crummy notch can prevent your getting a fire. So make it right! Here's how: Cut the notch in the shape of a triangle. The top point of the triangle is almost to the center of the hole. Carve out all the wood inside this triangle. The edges of the notch should flare from about 1/4 inch wide at the perimeter of the hole to 3/8 inch at the base of the triangle so the coal that forms can be easily tapped out of the notch. If the notch is too thin, dust might not accumulate in the notch but will form instead around the edges of the hole. To get the coal, you need the heat of friction and enough accumulation of dust. A thin notch also won't allow enough air in for the coal to form. This is also true for holes too far away from the edge of the board. On the other hand, too wide a notch means you have to drill until a week from next Tuesday to get enough dust to fill the darn thing. And if the notch is too wide, the drill will spin out of the hole and into the notch, slipping off the board!

Starting the friction fire. Once the notch is cut, get ready, because the

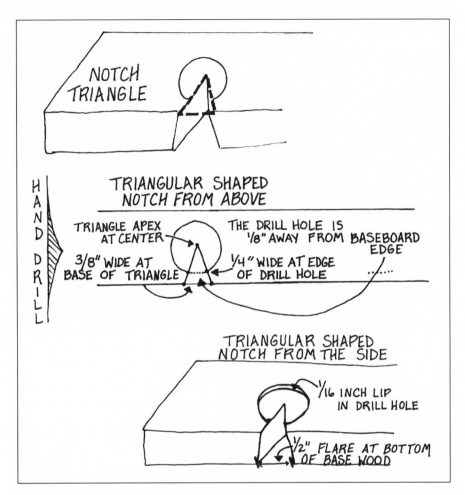

hundred-yard dash is about to begin. This game is about speed and pressure. Before you start, put a leaf or wood chip under the notch to catch the coal. Some people want to put the tinder under the notch, but the tinder fills up the notch and prevents air from getting where it needs to be. Besides, it's very hard to hold the base wood steady with a wad of tinder stuffed underneath it.

Now, start spinning the drill. Don't go full speed the first couple of passes down the drill, but do use good downward pressure so glaze doesn't form on the base. (Read about glaze in the fire-plow description.) Going slower initially lets you warm up as the wood heats up. Keep breathing, as your muscles need the air for this effort. You'd be surprised how many people need to be reminded to breathe! After those first couple of passes, increase speed and maintain good downward pressure.

Note that with softwoods such as cedar, cottonwood, and clematis, speed and smoothness may be more important than brute pressure. Intense pressure can send the drill plumb through these softwood bases before the coal has a chance to form. If this happens, try decreasing pressure. If that doesn't work, try a wider drill or a softer wood for the drill. But if you are using a sage base and a mullein drill, pressure is everything. Otherwise that shiny black or brown glaze will build up and decrease friction. If there is no smoke after a few passes, or if you start hearing a squawking sound, you should look for that sinister glaze and act accordingly. If the glaze forms, bearing down hard will cut through it; however, it is much easier to stop and scrape off the glaze with a sharp stone or put some dry sand in the hole and drill it off. Sometimes with a mullein drill, we have had a small glazed cap form in the central pith of the stalk. This is a problem because it acts like a bearing. If you experience this when using a pithy drill, carve or pop the cap off with a knife and hollow the pith out slightly.

It is important that the drill not pop out of the hole while you are drilling because this will cool everything off quickly and delay the formation of the coal; so, keep steady when drilling. Also, be aware that the drill can pop out when you have spun your hands down to the bottom of the drill and need to go back up. To avoid this, stop both hands at the bottom of the drill and keep the drill in the hole with one hand while moving the other quickly to the top. Then join it with the second hand and quickly drill down again. If you are doing this with a buddy, the other person should start drilling when you reach the bottom.

If you continue to have trouble getting enough downward pressure, try these two ideas: 1) When we first started making hand-drill fires, the second person held a rock with a hole in it against the top of the drill to give downward pressure; try that, or 2) use the method John McPherson showed us. To the top of the drill, attach the center of a thong that has a loop at each side for your thumbs. Insert thumbs, and drill. Your hands will stay up on the shaft, and you can and should use a shorter shaft so the downward pressure exerted by the thong won't snap the shaft. When you want a break, keep your thumbs in the loops but spread out your hands and let another person spin the drill. You will be applying the downward pressure, and they can drill like crazy and give *your* muscles a rest.

Once the dust that is spilling into the notch has started smoking on its

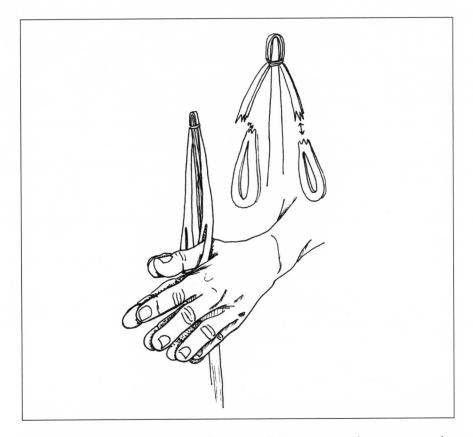

own, you can be pretty sure you have a coal. But wait until you are sure the smoke is coming from the coal-dust pile and not from the drill. No wishful thinking. Every time you stop to check, you cool off the set and make your job harder. (By the way, the dust comes from the two woods rubbing together and breaking down. If one wood is softer than the other, your dust will be primarily of this softwood.)

So, now you really see that independent wisp of smoke coming from the coal-dust pile? OK! Stop drilling and gently lift the drill out of the hole. Take a breath! You've worked hard to get a coal. It would be a shame to lose it now by rushing, so go slow here.

Carefully lift the front of the baseboard a little and knock it with your knuckle to loosen the coal from the notch. Now, slowly pick up the wood chip or leaf that the coal is on and dump the coal into the fine dust stuffed into the center of the tinder nest. Blow the tinder nest to a flame. Congratulations!

BOW-DRILL METHOD

Now, if the paleolithic pedagogue comes around to quiz you on fire methods and then bids you choose only one method for the rest of your life, be sure to answer this ancient tutor thus: the **bow drill.** This method is very reliable, even in damp weather, as you have tremendous mechanical advantage with a rock to hold down the drill and a bow instead of your hands to spin the drill. However, it takes more coordination to use a bow-drill set, and it takes a lot longer to whittle a bow-drill set than to prepare a fire-plow or hand-drill set. It's not as primal as the fire plow or as sexy as the hand drill. Nevertheless, for reliability, choose a bow drill.

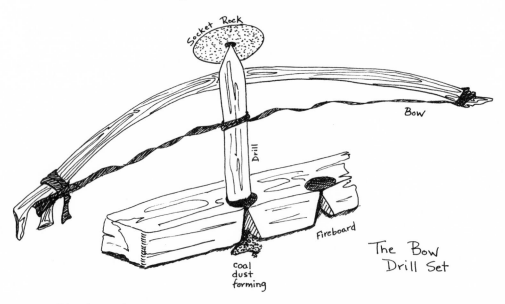

The Bow Drill Set

Woods we have used successfully in the bow-drill method are sage, cottonwood, cedar, yucca, willow, elderberry, and alder. Pine has not worked for us. Experiment with your local woods.

Here's how to make a bow-drill set. The baseboard should be wider than the drill. It's good to make the base wide enough to have two rows of holes. The board will last a long time this way, and if you choose a hardwood such as sage for the baseboard, you'll be glad to get a lot of fires from it before carving a new base. Make the base 2 inches **x** 8 inches **x** 1/2 inch thick.

The drill dimensions can vary. The smaller the diameter of the drill, the faster it will spin. But if it is too thin or too long, it may snap under the sideways pressure from the bow. A thin drill may also drill too quickly into the

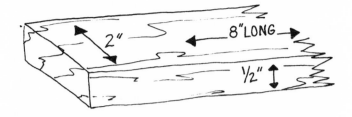

board, burning through before a coal is formed. A good width to start out with is 3/4 inch. The drill will wear down quickly at both ends, so don't start with too short a drill. We love foot-long sage drills when we can find pieces that are straight enough. However, 8 inches is a good length. Once the drill gets shorter than 3 inches, holding it steady with the rock gets more difficult.

The top of the drill should be sharply pointed so it can spin freely in the rock without slipping out. The bottom of the drill should be fairly flat. This provides maximum friction between the drill and the base, ensuring plenty of dust and heat. Remember, though, when you first drill in the hole to set the drill and carve a notch, it's easier if the bottom of the drill is slightly pointed so it will stay in the hole you have gouged in the baseboard. You can flatten the drill bottom if you need to after you carve your notch.

The bow that spins the drill should be about 1 foot 8 inches long, with a natural bend. Make sure it is long enough so you can take full strokes that allow your arm to fully extend in front of you. It is good to have a bow that is dry and doesn't flex much. This will help keep the bowstring tension constant.

A fork on the end of the bow where you hold it is ideal. You can just wind the string around the fork to secure it instead of tying it down under your hand. The string stretches as it gets hot, and this fork allows you to adjust the tightness of the string easily without untying and retying it for each adjustment. Carve a notch for the string at the far end of the bow.

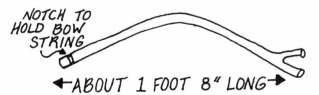

Our favorite material for a bowstring is a strip of buckskin 3/4 inch wide that has been twisted to a round cord. It grips the drill nicely without having to be overly tight. And it doesn't melt like nylon cord if the string is slipping on the drill. Tie the cord around the notches at the far end of the bow, and wrap it around the fork at the end you will hold. Gripping your hand around the wrapped buckskin cord will keep it from coming undone.

STRING FOR BOW 3/4" WIDE

Test the tension of your bow string when putting in the drill. It should be tight, but not *so* tight that you break the bow or the string while putting it around the drill. Still, the cord needs to be tight enough so that you feel tension when you twist the drill into the string.

You will need a rock or something else to hold the drill steady and apply downward pressure on the drill. The rock should fit comfortably in your hand. Soft sandstone is easy to grind a hole in with a harder rock. Almost any stone you can make a hole in works well. Exceptions would be something like pumice, which is so soft that a drill would bore right through it. Some rocks will have ready-made holes. A piece of hardwood will work instead of a rock, but the top of the drill can smoke and bind in the hole. Knee bones of deer and elk are small and harder to hold but have holes in them already. Some shells will work too. Whatever you use, make sure the hole is deep enough. The problem most people have with the rock is that the hole is so shallow

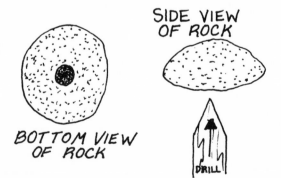

SIDE VIEW
OF ROCK

BOTTOM VIEW
OF ROCK

DRILL

that when the drill point wears down, or the weary or inexperienced bow driller tilts the rock a little too much, the drill pops out, flying into the back forty!

Getting ready. So, now you have all the pieces of the bow-drill set. Start by drilling a hole and carving a notch for the coal dust. First, gouge an indentation in the base wood where you will spin the drill. You need to place this gouge on the base so that when you spin the drill, the drill edge is no more than 1/4 inch from the edge of the baseboard. If these directions sound familiar, it's because you did this for the hand-drill set too, but your dimensions for the hand drill were smaller.

To do this, put the arch of your foot down over the board just next to the hole. The knee of your other leg will be on the ground, back behind you and out of the way of your bow. Twist the drill into the string so it is on the outside of the string, away from the bow. If the drill is on the inside of the string, closest to the bow, it can rub against the bow and make drilling more difficult. Put the bottom of the drill in the baseboard hole. Place the rock on the point of the drill. Hold the rock securely in your hand and brace your

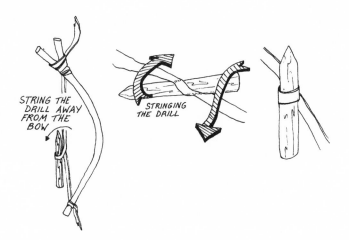

STRING THE DRILL AWAY FROM THE BOW

STRINGING THE DRILL

wrist against your shin, having your elbow on the outside of your leg. Pretend your wrist bone is melded to your shin bone during the drilling process.

When all is stable, slowly start sawing the bow back and forth. If the set is well made and your form is correct, smoke should come quickly, within the first 30 seconds. Drill till the hole is 1/8 inch deep and about as wide as the drill. Stop and cut the notch 3/8 inch wide at the perimeter of the hole and 5/8 inch wide at the base of the triangle. Make the notch almost to the middle; flare it at the bottom. Follow the same procedure as described for carving the notch in the hand-drill section.

Now is the time to fine-tune your bow-drill set. Is the baseboard flat and steady? Is the drill very pointed on top? Is the rock hole deep

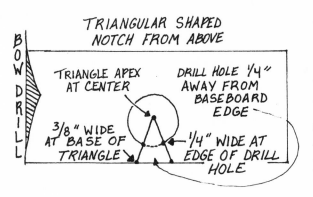

TRIANGULAR SHAPED NOTCH FROM ABOVE

BOW DRILL

TRIANGLE APEX AT CENTER

DRILL HOLE 1/4" AWAY FROM BASEBOARD EDGE

3/8" WIDE AT BASE OF TRIANGLE

1/4" WIDE AT EDGE OF DRILL HOLE

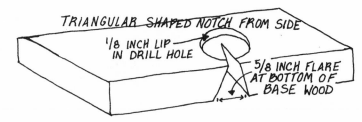

TRIANGULAR SHAPED NOTCH FROM SIDE

1/8 INCH LIP IN DRILL HOLE

5/8 INCH FLARE AT BOTTOM OF BASE WOOD

enough? Is the bowstring tight enough? Is the drill straight enough? If you answer "no" to any of these questions, STOP and fix it now.

Troubleshooting. There are a lot of parts to the bow-drill set. This means you have to pay more attention to detail. Let's look at these details before you start drilling for a coal, then you can troubleshoot quickly if problems arise in the process. The string should remain on the lower third of the drill to keep it from riding up the drill and popping the drill out from under the rock. If the string starts to slip on the drill, you can often keep drilling and correct this by tightening the string with a pinch of the thumb and forefinger or by holding the bow further up and gripping the string more firmly against the bow. If this doesn't work in mid-action, stop and adjust the string tension.

If you are having problems with the string breaking before you can get a coal, it is because the string rubs against itself at the drill and wears through. Although awkward, the cure for this problem is to tilt your end of the bow as you drill so the string doesn't contact itself around the drill.

The bow should not drag in, or dig into, the dirt or it will slow you down. You will avoid this by keeping the bow handle on a level plane.

The biggest challenges for beginners are endurance, holding the rock steady, the string slipping on the drill, and not enough downward pressure on the drill. Once these challenges are met, the rest comes pretty easily. A steadying hand from a friend can really cheer up a weary bow driller and assure a warm fire.

Now, let's make the fire! Here comes the real thing. Do you have a tinder nest? Is your kindling ready? OK! Put a leaf or wood chip under the notch to hold the coal, and start drilling. Keep the rock and drill steady. Meld that wrist bone to the shinbone. If the string loosens, pinch it with your thumb and forefinger and keep drilling long fast strokes. Keep breathing; *you* need oxygen too. Apply good downward pressure. Use your upper body weight to press down on the rock but keep it steady! Go! Go! Go!

Stop when the dust pile is smoking on its own. Transfer the coal into the tinder nest and blow the nest to a flame.

These are three tried-and-true friction fire methods that we have taught to over a thousand people. You can do it! Keep practicing. The magic of creating fire is in your grasp.

CHAPTER

11

ROPE STRING THREAD

N O MATTER WHERE YOU LIVE, WHAT YOU DO, OR WHO YOU ARE, you rely on some kind of cord every day. From clothing to clothes lines, nets to nylons, tow ropes to tie downs—in every corner of your house you will find something woven, knitted, spun, corded, or braided. Spinning fibers in the Stone Age was an important industry, something everyone knew. Learning how to process plant and animal fiber today is fun, easy, and practical. Serviceable cord can be made from rags, paper towels, and even wire. But in this chapter we will focus on natural materials that can be easily obtained and prepared.

Making a cord from short fibers merely involves spinning, plying, or braiding them together to form a longer length. Once you understand this simple process, you can make the finest sewing thread or even a tow rope.

Let's start with finding fibers. We will divide this into two groups: animal and vegetable.

VEGETABLE FIBERS

Vegetable fiber is generally not as strong as animal, but it is easy to find and actually increases in strength under wet conditions. The materials you choose must be flexible enough to twist and bend without breaking, yet still be strong enough to hold up in the task you are doing. Vegetable fibers are not only stronger when wet, but they often spin and cord better wet.

When you collect fibers, make sure you're within the local laws. In our community, we can't collect from local parks but roadsides are OK.

Many plants yield usable fibers. Here are some we have used: inner bark from flax, dogbane, milkweed, stinging nettle, black walnut, Osage orange, elm, basswood, willow, big leaf sage, and cliff rose. We have also used yucca, cattail, tulle, and iris leaves, palm fronds, coconut husks, corn husks, and grass. Experiment with plants in your region.

Dogbane is our local favorite. We collect it in early October, just when it turns from green to rust. It can be collected later, but the longer it is exposed to the weather, the weaker it becomes. It grows in low places where water runs or stands, and it is often found near cattails. It has narrow, pointed seedpods that hang downward. These pods, along with the branches at the top, give it a more bushy appearance than willow and, with practice, one can identify it while traveling at highway speeds. Since dogbane is a perennial, we cut it off at ground level. This way the root can keep spreading and sending up more stalks. Then we scatter the seedpods as well. Tying the stalks on the top of the car is a good way to scatter seed too!

Dogbane

Preparing the fiber. The following directions are for pithy plants such as dogbane, milkweed, and nettle.

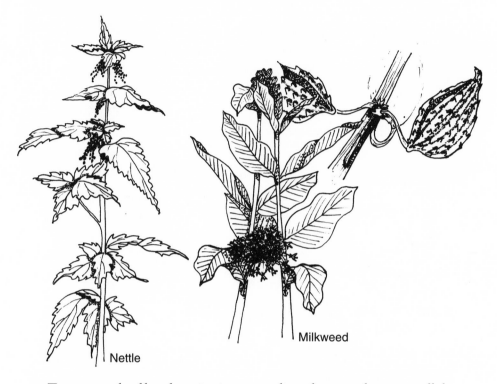

Milkweed

Nettle

To prepare the fiber for spinning or cording, first, gently scrape off the outer bark with a knife. Next, step on the stalks to flatten them. Do this gently on a flat surface so they break lengthwise in quarters but not into segmented lengths. Pick up the stalks and split them open, then in half lengthwise so you have four long quarters.

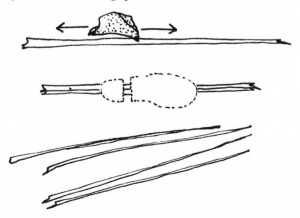

In preparation to peel the fiber off the hard inner stalk, hold two quartered lengths in your hand, grasping the wider bottom with the top of the stalk down (1). Have the inner pith of the stalk facing you. Hold the stalk about an inch from the end and gently break the woody stalk away from you. Do not break the fibers (2). Peel the bottom of the piece of broken stalk off the fiber by pulling upward. Now you have an inch of fiber sticking up (3). Grasp these fibers and peel them away from you and downward by pulling them over the forefinger of your hand that is holding the stalk (4). If you support the fibers with the back of your forefinger this way, they will have less chance of breaking.

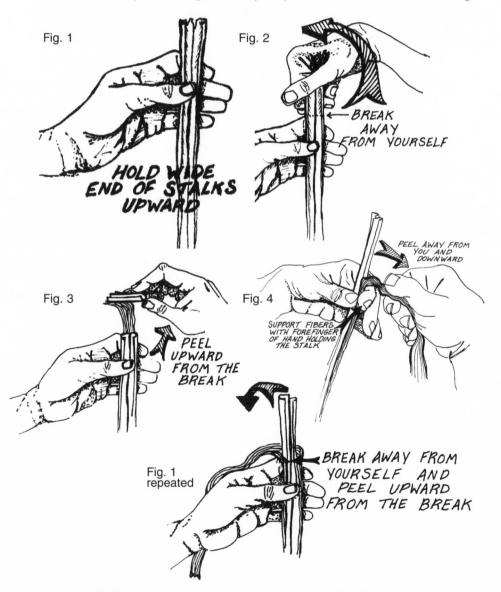

Fig. 1 — HOLD WIDE END OF STALKS UPWARD

Fig. 2 — ← BREAK AWAY FROM YOURSELF

Fig. 3 — PEEL UPWARD FROM THE BREAK

Fig. 4 — PEEL AWAY FROM YOU AND DOWNWARD — SUPPORT FIBERS WITH FOREFINGER OF HAND HOLDING THE STALK

Fig. 1 repeated — BREAK AWAY FROM YOURSELF AND PEEL UPWARD FROM THE BREAK

Peel back an inch or two of fiber and stop. Gently break the stalk again, just above your gripping finger, and peel it away from the fibers as before. Then peel fibers backward and downward, with finger support, stopping every two or three inches to repeat the steps. If you decide to rush things and simply rip the fiber down the stalk, the fiber will quickly taper and break off. Don't do it.

Now, set aside the length of fiber you have just stripped and pick up the other half of the stalk. When you have removed the fibers from this half, lay the wider ends of this fiber onto the thinner ends of the fibers from the other half of the stalk. This makes the overall thickness of the fibers consistent. Gently twist these together and wrap the fiber in a coil for storage and set aside.

Go on to the next plant. Once you have enough fiber for your project, either wet the fibers and start spinning, or if you want extra-soft cordage, gently buff the fibers between your hands or hold an inch between thumbs and forefingers and rotate your fingers like pedaling a bike. Go up and down the full length of the fiber. This will remove any remaining outer bark, leaving just the soft inner bark with high-quality fibers.

Some plants such as flax and yucca are best after they've rotted a little to aid in removal of the fibers. For flax, keep the stalks outside and wet them down daily. Test to see when the fibers slough off easily. If you let them rot too long, you won't have fiber! So check often. For yucca, pound the leaves between smooth stones and soak anywhere from a few days to two weeks, or as long as it takes for the cellulose to separate from the fibers by gently working them in your hands in the water. The water should be changed periodically, especially if it gets smelly or slimy. (Use the first clean pour-off for a bubble bath; see Chapter 8 on soap.) This process will yield softer fibers. You may need to scrape away the cellulose after soaking before stripping apart the fibers.

Yucca can also be used without soaking, but the cord will be stiff and coarse. Cut the leaves, a few from each plant. Scrape the fleshy part of the leaf away with a knife while holding the leaf on a flat surface. If you do it against your leg, slivers of the leaves will go into your leg, even through clothing! Separate the fibers by splitting them apart lengthwise. They can be dried for later use. When you are ready to use them again, soak the dry fibers until they are pliable.

You can use yucca for sewing without even cording or spinning it. The spike at the tip of each leaf makes a great needle. Cut straight down into the leaf on each side of the spike. Grasp the spike and peel. The center fibers between your two cuts will peel away from the leaf. You'll have a needle with the thread already attached.

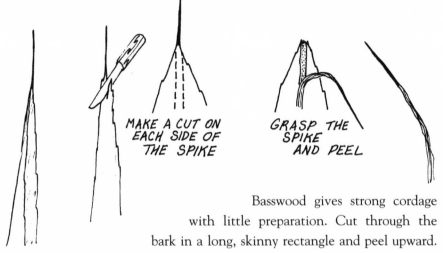

MAKE A CUT ON
EACH SIDE OF
THE SPIKE

GRASP THE
SPIKE
AND PEEL

Basswood gives strong cordage with little preparation. Cut through the bark in a long, skinny rectangle and peel upward. Don't go all around the tree or it will die. Separate the inner bark into strips of desired thickness and spin, cord, or lash. If you allow it to rot in water a bit so that the bulky cellulose will slough off, the resulting fibers will be very strong.

We use black walnut, elm, and Osage orange wood for making bows. The inner bark of these trees, when wet, makes fine cord, too. Once the bark dries, it becomes more brittle but still works well for lashing. We use willow for baskets and have tried the wet bark for cord. It is weak but will work for some applications that don't require a lot of strength.

ANIMAL FIBERS

Fibers from animals that can be used for making cord can come from the outside or the inside of the animal. Wool works better than hair because it grips onto itself and is softer and finer. Hair will work, but it helps to first coat it with wax or pitch to keep it from untwisting.

Sinew, the body part that connects muscle to bone and encases muscles, makes strong cord and thread. The longest fibers come from along the backbone and also from the Achilles tendon. For sewing, back sinew works best because it is long, sometimes three feet long if you get it from an elk. (Deer has finer sinew than elk, but not as long.) Just strip the sinew into threads while it is fresh; then either use it wet or dry it for storage. Rehydrate it before use. Dried leg sinew that is not separated into usable strands while fresh will need to be pounded between wood or *smooth* rocks to separate the fibers. Then they can be stripped apart. Pounded sinew is a little weaker, but sometimes the loss of strength is worth the trade-off of being able to store it dry in whole-tendon form.

For lashing, sinew should be wet. It will shrink during drying for a tight lash. But for cording it is easier to work with dry sinew since it is slick when wet.

Sinew makes great thread for sewing moccasins. It is good for clothing too, but it must be sewn in such a way that the seams cover the stitching because when sinew dries, it feels like monofilament fishing line, and this roughness can make you itch. (See Chapter 12 for sewing methods.) Sinew is strong when kept dry. As a cord or rope, it is not the best choice for wet conditions because the splices will slip. For sewing moccasins or other leather clothing, wet sinew is fine. The leather supports the splices and keeps them from unraveling or slipping.

Spinning Fibers

Now that you have some material to work with, either vegetable or animal, you can start with simple spinning. This will give you a product that can be knitted, woven, or braided.

Fibers should be prepared so that they are fine and soft. Working them back and forth in the hands or buffing them as described before will accomplish this. Buffing also gives more surface area for the fibers to grip into each other.

Hold the ends of the fibers in one hand and twist the fibers together. As they twist they will form a yarnlike product. It may be faster to spin this by laying the fibers on your leg. Holding one end up with slight tension, roll the fibers with your other hand down the length of your thigh. When the fibers start to thin, add some more. It may help to wet the fibers before working. Drop spindles are also a simple way to spin longer fibers. With practice, you will be able to achieve consistent thickness. It is a good idea to roll up your spun fiber as you make it since it will want to tangle or, worse, untwist and separate.

Making Cord

The next step is making a cord that doesn't want to untwist. Cord is good for rope, sewing thread, netting, and general use. But it is not very appropriate for weaving on a loom since hand-plied cord is bumpy, and it is hard to compact the woven strands together to form a really tight cloth. The cording method is called the *two-ply reverse wrap*. In this method, the twisted strands oppose each other, actually keeping each other from unraveling. Here's how to do it:

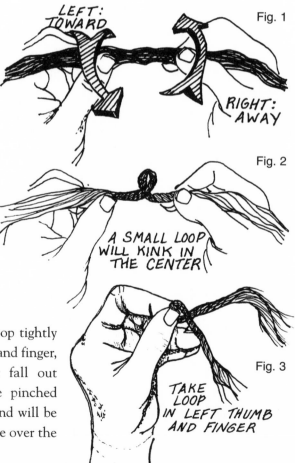

LEFT: TOWARD

RIGHT: AWAY

Fig. 1

Fig. 2

A SMALL LOOP WILL KINK IN THE CENTER

Fig. 3

TAKE LOOP IN LEFT THUMB AND FINGER

1. Grasp the prepared fibers firmly between your thumbs and forefingers. Place both thumbs and forefingers about an inch apart. With the right thumb and forefinger, twist tightly away from you. At the same time, with the left thumb and forefinger, twist tightly toward you.

2. As you do this, a small loop will kink in the center of the fiber.

3. Pinch this little loop tightly between your left thumb and finger, letting strands of fiber fall out toward the right of the pinched loop. (The hindmost strand will be on top. Your thumb will be over the

loop when doing this, so the strands stick out from your thumb. The strand that appears on top, or above the other, is actually the one behind the other.)

4. Twist the top and behind strand tightly away from you.

5. When it is tightly twisted, bring it toward you and lay it in front and below the untwisted bottom strand of fiber.

6. Now this first twisted fiber is the new bottom strand (actually in front). Go to the new "top" untwisted strand and twist it tightly away from you.

7. When it is good and tight, bring it toward you and lay it in front and below the bottom strand. Alternate and repeat until your cord is finished. As you work, you'll need to move your left thumb and finger slowly along the forming cord.

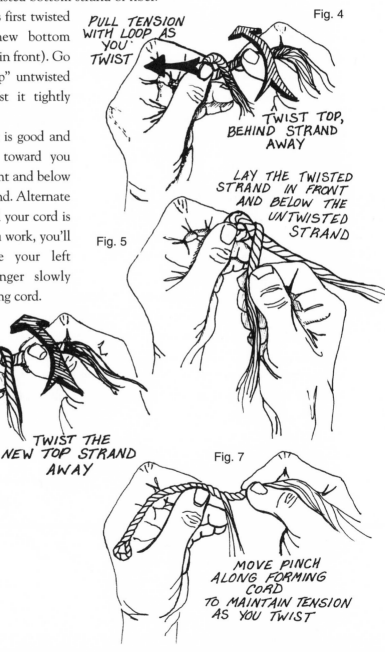

Fig. 4

PULL TENSION WITH LOOP AS YOU TWIST

TWIST TOP, BEHIND STRAND AWAY

LAY THE TWISTED STRAND IN FRONT AND BELOW THE UNTWISTED STRAND

Fig. 5

Fig. 6

TWIST THE NEW TOP STRAND AWAY

Fig. 7

MOVE PINCH ALONG FORMING CORD TO MAINTAIN TENSION AS YOU TWIST

If you keep your pinch near where the twist is happening, you can get better tension to make a tight twist. Remember, however, this pinch is *not* holding the cord together. The cording process allows the fibers to hold together on their own. The pinch keeps good tension.

As the fibers start to thin out or get too short, splice in fiber for new length or thickness. Just lay the new fiber over the old and roll them together in the simple spinning process. Give splices a lot of overlap so you'll have a strong cord. And if the end of the splice is thick, taper it so the resulting cord will be smooth.

The two-ply reverse wrap is easy and relatively strong. For a stronger cord, *three plies* are the way to go. Start as with two plies, but add an additional ply in the beginning. This extra ply will make a cord that is rounder and stronger.

When strong cord is important for the job you are doing, you'll want to check the quality and strength of your cord as you make it. Here's how: Pinch the thumbs and fingers of both hands, about one inch apart, on the section of the cord you want to test. Rotate your thumbs and fingers in opposite directions to untwist the cord. Look closely at the strands of each ply. The tensioned, untwisted plies *must* both be straight instead of one straight and the other slack, curving up or down. If they are not equally loaded (not both straight), then the resulting cord will have only half its potential strength. Do this test in various spots up and down the length of the cord. If you're using the cord for a fishing line, bowstring, or holding your tent down in a gale, you'll want equal tension. Also, keeping all plies equally thick as you cord will go a long way in solving this problem. Keep practicing. It doesn't take long to get high-quality cord.

If you are making thread, lay the fibers of your splice so the thinnest ends join into the corded fibers first. This way, when the thread is being pulled through a needle or hole, the splices won't catch and unravel or fuzz up.

SPLICING FOR THREAD

Once the cordage is made, if it will be subject to water or wet weather, rub it with runny pine pitch and then with a little rendered fat to keep the pitch from sticking to you and everything else. If mice will be sniffing around, omit the last step, as they will eat the cord to get the fat. You could also soak it in pitch varnish (see Chapter 10 on glue).

Finished cord, thread, or rope can be knotted with an overhand knot to keep the ends from unraveling before use.

LACING

Lacing of various widths can be cut from buckskin and rawhide. These lacings can be used as they are, or you can cord or braid them for stronger rope or lashing.

Cut around and around the outside of the rawhide or buckskin to make long, unbroken lengths. Then wet it and stretch it before cording or braiding.

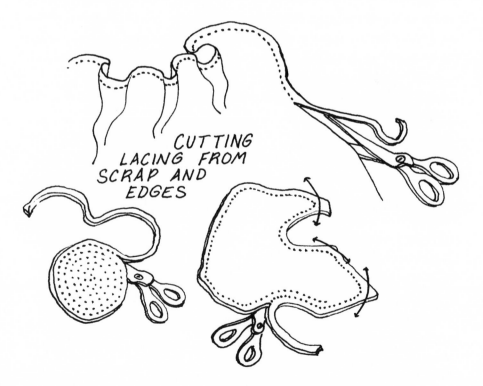

CUTTING LACING FROM SCRAP AND EDGES

Splice buckskin and rawhide by cutting a slit 1/4 inch from the end of both pieces. The cuts should look like the letter "T." Then insert the uncut ends of both pieces of lacing into the slit of the other piece. Pull tight. It will look similar to a square knot but without loose ends.

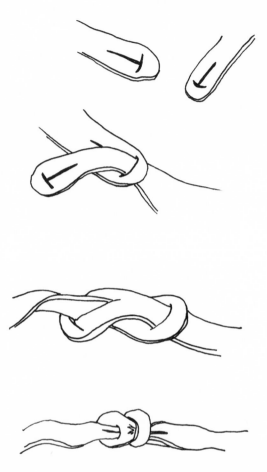

Remember, all animal fibers will shrink as they dry. This is great when you're lashing down something, unless you ever want to untie it! You can even increase this holding power by soaking animal fibers in hide glue and then doing the lashing. (See Chapter 10 on glue.) Once the lashing dries, cover it with pitch if it will be exposed to rain or snow. Otherwise, just keep it dry, and it will hold till the buffalo come home!

BRAIDING

We have all seen braids—the simple weaving of three bunches of hair back and forth. It doesn't take much imagination to see that a braid could make a useful rope, as Rapunzel showed us. A rope that is braided has less tendency to twist and kink than a rope that is constructed by twisting. Hawaiians braid plant fibers into heavy-duty ropes for use at sea. They leave coconut husks in the salt water to rot; then when only the rot-resistant fibers are left, they first spin those and then braid them.

The strongest ropes we have made have a four-braid core covered by a four-braid sheath. If you want to make a very strong rope (for a dog leash, for instance), make a four-braided core first.

Cut two *long* strands of leather or rawhide. (You can always splice for

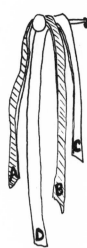

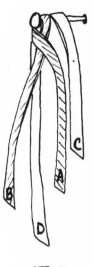

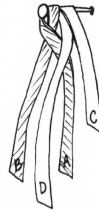

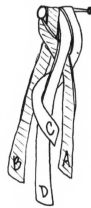

additional length.) Wet and stretch the two strands. This lessens the amount of stretch in the final rope.

Fold the strands so you have four ends hanging down. Follow the pictures to braid in the four-braid style. At first, it may be helpful to label the strands like the pictures to keep from getting mixed up.

Once the core is made as long as you want it, you can use it as it is or cover it for added strength. Let the core dry before covering it.

The width of the strands of the cover braid must equal the circumference of the core so there are no gaps. So, if the core is 2 inches around, each strand of the cover should be 1/2 inch wide. Wet and stretch the strands before trimming them to 1/2 inch. Follow the same four-braid directions.

Three-strand flat braids work well for fiber sandal lacing, belts, bag straps, and shoulder straps on packs.

NETTING

Because nets are lightweight and strong, they are very useful. Every culture has used them for various tasks and pleasures. There is nothing as satisfying as kicking back in a hammock you made yourself and drifting off to sleep with a gentle breeze for a lullaby. Besides hammocks, uses for net in the modern

world are just as endless as they were for your ancestors—from basketball nets to hangers for potted plants, from shopping bags to fishnets.

The best netting knot is a *sheet bend*. It's a little tricky to learn, but once you have it, you could do it in your sleep—and believe me, once you start, your cord maker will have to work overtime to keep up with you.

Here we'll explain nets made in a circle (for uses such as shopping bags, plant holders, and cast nets) and nets made in a rectangle (for hammocks, hockey goals, or hunting nets).

To first learn netting, start off by making a *shuttle* to hold the cord. The simplest shuttle to start with is made by using a green stick 1/2 inch in diameter and 10 inches long. Split both ends of the stick down 1 inch. Wrap the cord around the length of the stick, anchoring it into the splits.

A second type of shuttle can be made like the figure at the right. Use wood or bone. It should be 10 inches long and narrow so it will fit through the mesh. To load this shuttle with cord, first tie a slipknot around the middle point. Pull the cord down and

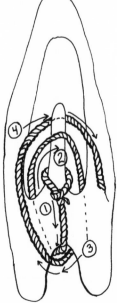

around the bottom of the shuttle and then back up and over the point on the other side. Alternate sides with every wrap.

While you learn to make the *netting knot,* use your fingers to space the mesh. Once you have the knot down, switch over to a wood or bone gauge instead of your fingers. Your netting will speed up and get more consistent with the gauge.

Make a few practice loops to imitate the bottom of mesh loops and hang them over nails spaced a couple inches apart. Make them out of anything you want and any size you want. You will practice making netting knots on the bottom of these loops. The drawings below and on the next page show how to make the knot:

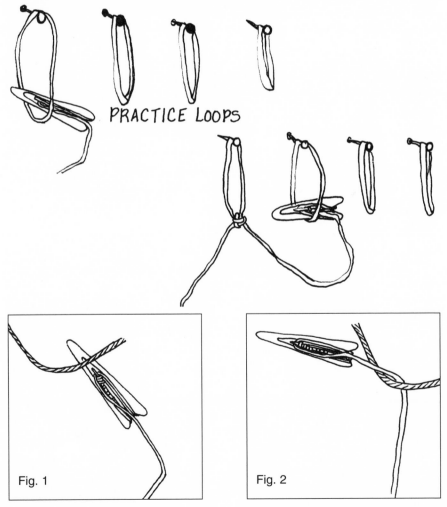

PRACTICE LOOPS

Fig. 1

Fig. 2

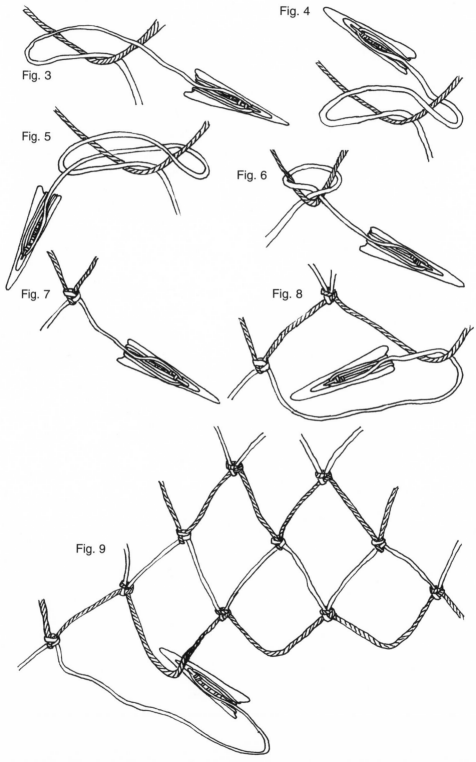

Fig. 3

Fig. 4

Fig. 5

Fig. 6

Fig. 7

Fig. 8

Fig. 9

Now you know the knot. You're ready to make a net.

First, make a gauge. To determine its size, decide what size you want your mesh. Measure the circumference of the mesh opening. Carve your gauge to have a circumference exactly one-half your mesh measurement. For example, if the mesh opening you want measures 4-1/2 inches total on all sides, then carve the gauge to be 2-1/4 inches total around the width of all four sides. The measures given here are good for a shopping bag. Meshes would be larger than this for a hammock, smaller for a purse. Whatever width you make your gauge, be sure it is not more than 1/4 inch thick. One-eighth inch thick is even better. This way, as you make the netting knot, you can easily pinch the lower bite of the mesh with your first or second finger. Too wide a gauge makes this task difficult. You want to be able to pinch this bite in place because it becomes a slipknot if the knot shifts down as you tighten it.

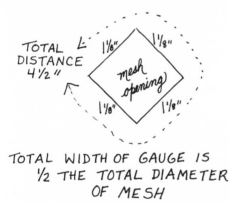

TOTAL DISTANCE 4 1/2 "   1 1/8"   1 1/8"   mesh opening   1 1/8"   1 1/8"

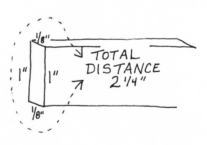

1/8"   TOTAL DISTANCE 2 1/4 "   1"   1"   1/8"

TOTAL WIDTH OF GAUGE IS 1/2 THE TOTAL DIAMETER OF MESH

Let's make a shopping bag. The start will be the same for any net. Here's the start:

Load your shuttle with as much cord as will allow the shuttle to pass through the mesh. Wrap the shuttle-cord tail twice around the gauge and tie a square knot. Leave a tail on the square knot twice as long as you want the finished bag. You will use this tail to complete each row, so don't forget it. When the cord runs out, connect it to the next piece with the netting knot or a square knot.

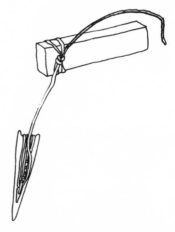

This first bit of double-wrapped cord is your first mesh. Slip the mesh off the gauge. Hang it on a nail so that the square knot is on the left side of the mesh, halfway between the nail and the bottom droop of the mesh. Pull the shuttle straight down from the knot, but don't let the square knot slip. Until you tie your first netting knot, you need to pay attention to keep the square knot in place (figure 1).

Loop the shuttle through the first mesh, cinch up the gauge, and prepare to make your second mesh. The gauge is your measure to get each mesh the same size. The distance from the nail to the square knot, the square knot to the bottom of the taut first mesh, and the width of your gauge should all be the same. These measurements are all one-half of your total mesh size (figure 2).

Bring the shuttle around the bottom of the gauge (figure 3).

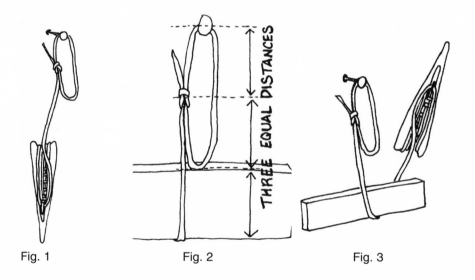

Fig. 1   Fig. 2   Fig. 3

Coming up from the right side, loop the shuttle through the first mesh from the back (figure 4).

After you bring the shuttle through, pull the shuttle down taut in front of the gauge. Remember to pull downward on the gauge with your other hand so it will cinch up against the bottom of the mesh (figure 5).

Bring the shuttle off to the left as it comes out of the mesh (figure 6).

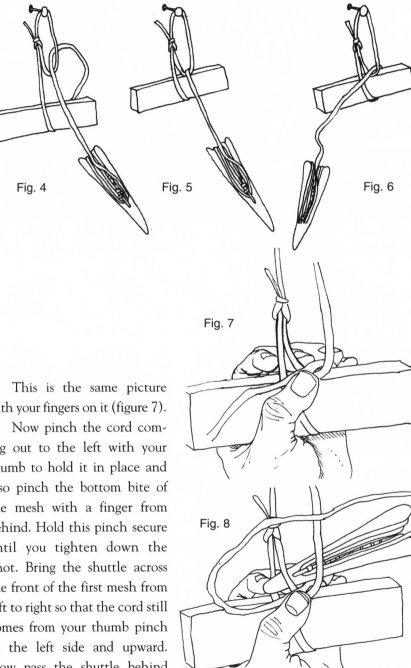

Fig. 4   Fig. 5   Fig. 6

Fig. 7

Fig. 8

This is the same picture with your fingers on it (figure 7).

Now pinch the cord coming out to the left with your thumb to hold it in place and also pinch the bottom bite of the mesh with a finger from behind. Hold this pinch secure until you tighten down the knot. Bring the shuttle across the front of the first mesh from left to right so that the cord still comes from your thumb pinch to the left side and upward. Now pass the shuttle behind the first two strings of the mesh from right to left (figure 8).

Shove the point of the shuttle forward and toward you after passing these two strings and bring the shuttle out in front of the third string, which is wrapped around the gauge. As the shuttle comes in front of this third string, keep pushing it forward and toward you through the loop you first made when keeping the cord pinched and off to the left. Pull the shuttle straight down to tighten (figure 9).

Keep that pinch secure! Keep pulling down to tighten while pinching (figure 10).

Here is a picture of how it tightens without your fingers in the way. You can see how it looks, but you should still be pinching the cords in place (figure 11).

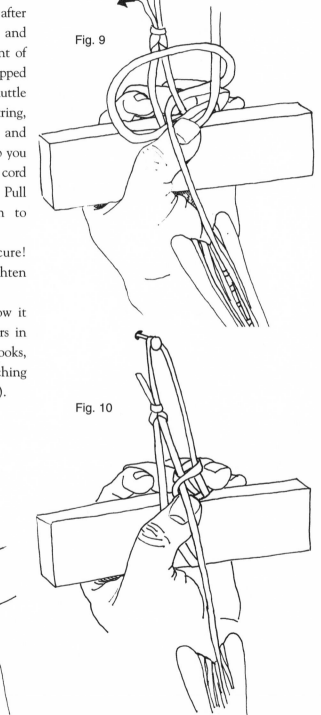

Fig. 9

Fig. 10

Fig. 11

Here is the complete knot (figure 12).

You can take your finger off now. This is what your start looks like so far (figure 13).

Take the gauge out of the second mesh (figure 14).

Flip the mesh to the right side (figure 15).

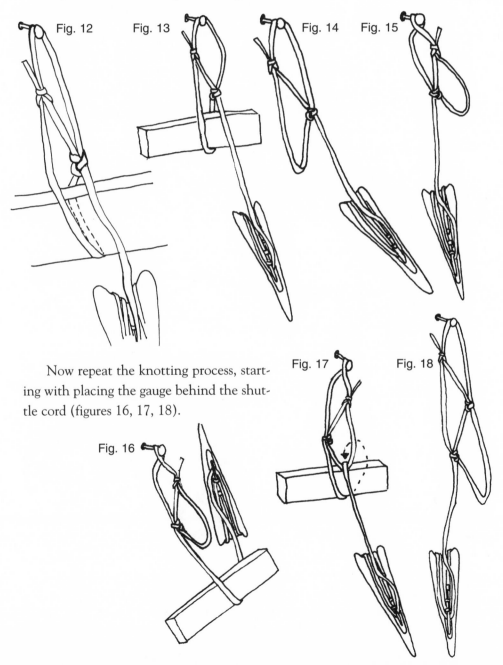

Fig. 12   Fig. 13   Fig. 14   Fig. 15

Fig. 16   Fig. 17   Fig. 18

Now repeat the knotting process, starting with placing the gauge behind the shuttle cord (figures 16, 17, 18).

After you make each new mesh, remove the gauge and flip the mesh so it is always on the right side. Flip to the right clockwise and then counter-clockwise every other time you finish a new mesh so your first mesh doesn't twist around and around the nail more and more tightly. You are making a mesh chain that will become the first two rows of your net (figure 19).

Fig. 19

For a shopping bag, continue this starting chain until you have about 40 meshes. When you have 40 meshes, take your starting chain off the nail and turn it horizontally so your original mesh, the one with the square knot and long tail, is on your left side and the square knot itself is at the bottom of the mesh. Lay the chain flat out on the floor (figure 20).

Fig. 20

Fig. 21

Make a long string that will become the handle of the bag. We like to use a four-braid cord. Weave this string in and out of the top row of mesh, starting with that square-knot mesh (figure 21).

When you pull the string through the final top-row mesh of the chain, tie the two ends of the string together. Hang this string on a nail. If you spread the chain out neatly, it will look like this (figure 22).

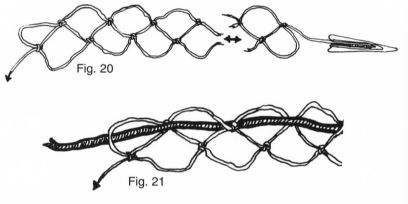

Fig. 22

The shuttle is loaded and coming off the end of the chain between the first and second rows of mesh. The square-knot tail hangs off the original first mesh and is ready to be tied to the cord coming off the

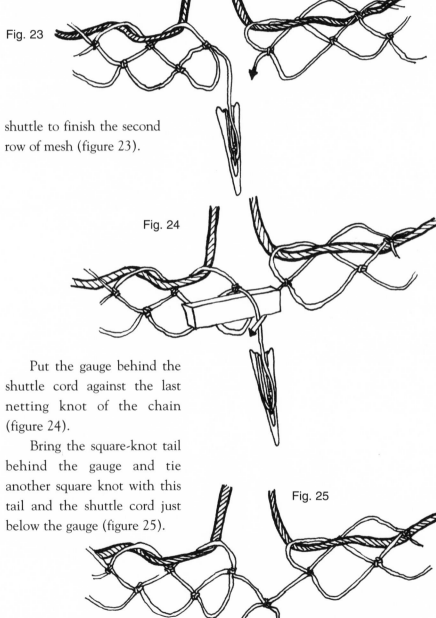

Fig. 23

shuttle to finish the second row of mesh (figure 23).

Fig. 24

Put the gauge behind the shuttle cord against the last netting knot of the chain (figure 24).

Bring the square-knot tail behind the gauge and tie another square knot with this tail and the shuttle cord just below the gauge (figure 25).

Fig. 25

Now you are ready to begin netting the third row of mesh. Work to the right and bring the shuttle through the bottom of the first mesh of the second row from back to front (figure 26). (You should be getting good at this by now!)

Put the gauge at the bottom of the mesh and tie the first netting knot of the third row (figure 27). Go all the way around the bag completing the third row until you come to your square-knot tail again. Now you will tie a square knot with the shuttle cord and the square-knot tail to finish the third row. Do it the same way as described for finishing the second row. You will notice that the square knots run in a diagonal down to the left (figure 28).

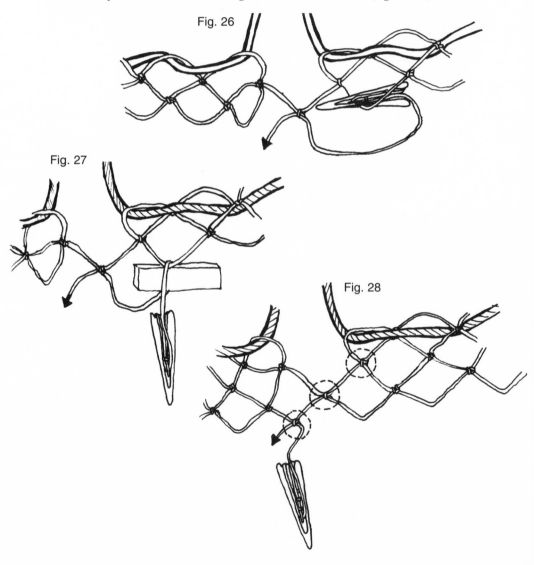

Fig. 26

Fig. 27

Fig. 28

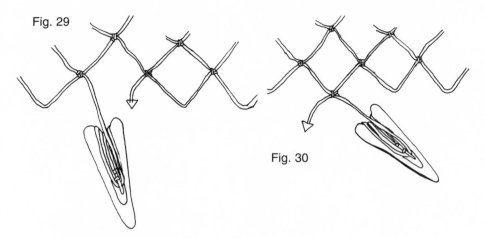

Fig. 29

Fig. 30

Continue netting for fifteen rows, finishing the last row with a final square knot (figure 29, 30).

Now you are ready to close up the bottom. Finish the bottom with netting knots just like you have been tying. But instead of going around in a straight line to make a row, zigzag back and forth on the bottom row of mesh. Make the first zigzag mesh to the right of the square knot. Make it small, with no droop in the bottom (figure 31).

Tie the netting knot. Pull the shuttle cord off to the left and go to the mesh on the left side of the square knot (figure 32).

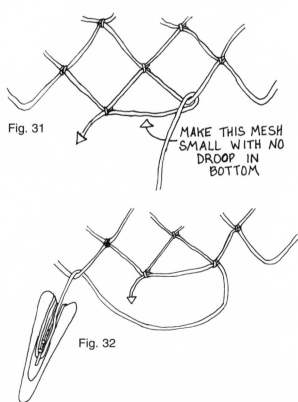

Fig. 31

MAKE THIS MESH SMALL WITH NO DROOP IN BOTTOM

Fig. 32

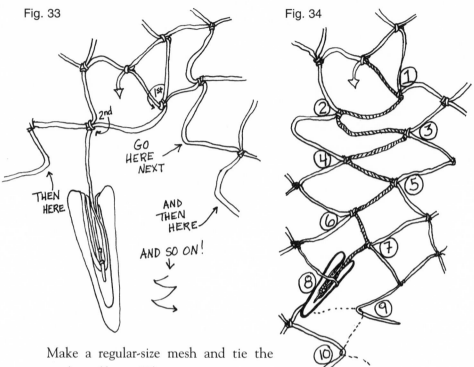

Fig. 33

Fig. 34

Make a regular-size mesh and tie the netting knot (figure 33).

Now, making regular-size meshes, zigzag back and forth along the bottom row until you are finished (figure 34). Tie a final netting knot. You have a shopping bag!

Other netting projects. If you don't want a basketball hoop, plant hanger, or shopping bag, maybe a hockey goal or a hammock are on your list. Decide how wide you want your project. Measure your mesh and gauge, and make your starting chain just as before. When it's finished, lay it on the floor and put a rod through the first row of the chain and hang it horizontally

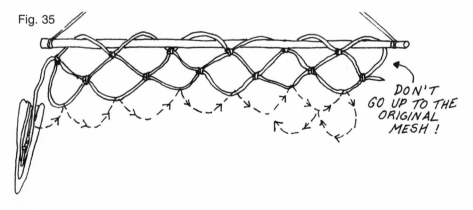

Fig. 35

(figure 35). Have the end of the chain so the loaded shuttle is hanging on the left side. This way you can net from left to right, just as you have learned. To start the third row, come down from the last netting knot and loop the shuttle through the final mesh of the chain (last mesh in second row). As you finish the third row, make sure you stop on the last mesh of the second row. Do not go up to the original mesh with the square knot. If you do this, your net will widen. Each row should have the same number of mesh. At the end of each new row, flip the rod over so the shuttle is once again on the left side; then begin netting the next row, once again from left to right. When the net is as long as you want it, you are finished.

CARD WEAVING

Card weaving is an ancient technique for making a strong strap quickly. A six-foot strap can be woven in a couple of hours. You don't need a loom, just cards with holes in the corners and about 200 feet of cord. If you're cording it yourself, you need to get busy! The cards can be made of cardboard, leather, rawhide, bark, wood, fired clay, or even stone.

A shuttle to hold the weft (the cord woven back and forth) is helpful but not necessary. You can use either netting shuttle described in the previous section or other shuttles described in Chapter 3 on tools.

We are going to give you directions to weave a strap that is strong enough for pack straps, basket handles, tumplines, and saddle cinches. If you do a pattern like the one we give directions for, then it will be lovely enough for curtain ties, belts, and other uses too.

The pattern explained here takes twelve cards and two colors of cord. If you don't want a pattern in the strap, just use all one color cord. This strap will be six feet long, but you can make it any length you want.

First make the cards. Cut 3-inch squares out of your chosen card material. The thinner the cards, the easier they are to rotate in the weaving. Make a hole in each of the four corners of all 12 cards. Leave room in the corner to label the cards where you can see the label as you work with the cards.

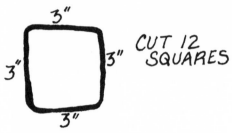

CUT 12 SQUARES

Labeling the cards is very important. Do it just this way. Lay all the cards in front of you and write the letter A in the top left-hand corner of each card. Now write B through D clockwise in each corner. When the letters are on the cards, number them 1 through 12 along the edge of the card between the letters D and A. Now place all the labeled cards in a stack so the numbers are on the top, facing you, with all the letters aligned. Put card number 1 on top of the stack, closest to you, and card number 12 on the bottom.

For this example, you will need 48, six-foot-long, warp cords (the cords that go through the cards). Twenty-two cords will be of a lighter color and twenty-six cords will be of a darker color. (We will use "lighter" and "darker" in our threading for a pattern description, so it will be

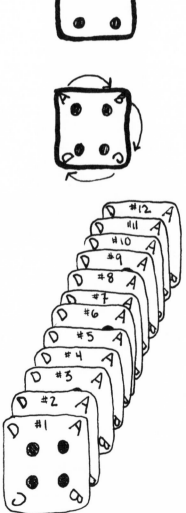

helpful if you cut them this way.) Lay the cords on the floor.

Now you are ready to thread the cards. For clarity in explaining how to thread the cards, the side with the letters and numbers is called the front side. The blank side is called the back.

Hold the stack of cards in your hand with all the numbers on top. Turn the fronts of the cards to the left, numbers still on top, so you are holding the stack sideways. Cards 1 through 6 will be threaded in their back side and out their front. Cards 7 through 12 will be threaded in their front side and out their back. Having half of the cards threaded from back to front and the other half of the cards threaded from front to back gives a balanced strap, one that will not want to twist when it is finished.

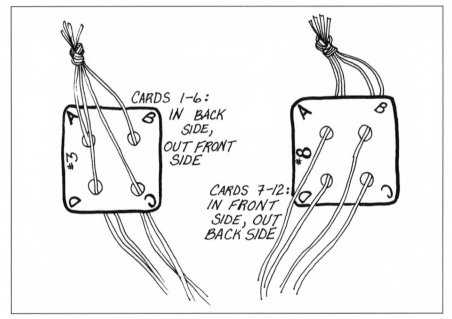

You have cut cords of lighter and darker color to make our favorite pattern that will give diamonds, arrowheads, Xs, and other symmetric shapes, depending on how you turn the cards. To get this pattern, you need to thread lighter and darker cords through the cards in a particular order described below. If you don't care about the pattern, you can thread these lighter and darker cords any way you want to through the holes of each card to get a random pattern, or, if you have all the same color cord, thread the cards as described above and skip the threading directions for making the pattern. Remember, whatever you decide about pattern, each card must be threaded with all four cords going from the front to the back or from the back to the front, in order for that card to be able to rotate properly.

Here is the threading pattern (remember to thread 1 through 6 from back to front):

Card 1: All holes are threaded with a dark color.

Card 2: All holes threaded with light color.

Card 3: A with dark, the rest light.

Card 4: A and B dark, C and D light.

Card 5: A, B, and C dark, D light.

Card 6: B light, A, C and D dark.

Card 7 (from now on, thread from front to back): B light, A, C and D dark.

Card 8: A, B, and C dark, D light.

Card 9: A and B dark, C and D light.

Card 10: A dark, B, C, and D light.

Card 11: All light.

Card 12: All dark.

After you thread each card, tie the ends of the four cords together in a knot. Push the card almost up to this knot. You should have almost six feet of cord between you and the card.

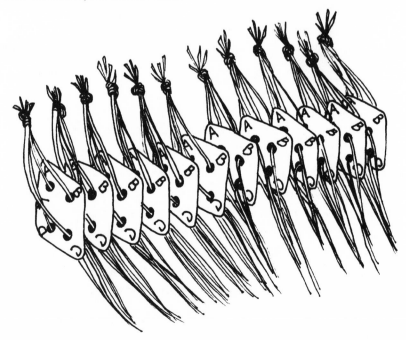

Now take the knotted ends of all the cords and tie them all together with a strong piece of string around the bottom of all the knots. Tie this strong string to something solid, such as a nail, a tree, or a door latch, at about eye level. Check your cards to make sure they are all turned up the same way. This will ensure the least amount of tangle. All the cards must be positioned with holes A and D on top, D in the left corner and A in the right corner, with the numbers center. To untangle the warp threads, gently pull all the cards away from their knotted ends toward you. It helps to have another pair of hands to untangle the cords as you pull the cards toward you. Pull the cards until they are one foot from the end of the cords. Comb this last foot with your fingers. Then pull the ends of all the cords together, under equal tension and tie the ends in an overhand knot. You can get the tension really equal if you slide the cards up and down a few times while pulling back on the ends before you tie the knot. Tie a strong string around the top of this knot. Now tie this end to your belt. Make sure it holds the warp cords under good tension. This makes it easier to weave.

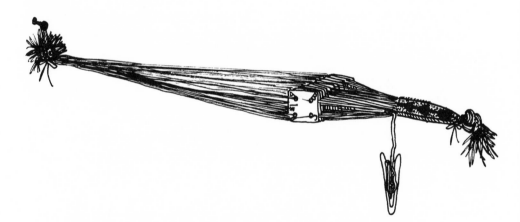

Load the shuttle with dark cord.

Now you're ready to start weaving. Check your cards. Are they all positioned with D in the left top corner, the number center top, and A in the right top corner? Good. Take all the cards in your hands and turn them, all at once, one quarter turn away from you so holes A and B are on top. Slide the cards back and forth until the warp splits into two sets of cords. This split is where you will run the shuttle through the warp.

When the split opens, use your hands to firmly pull the separating warps apart. Now pass the shuttle through this opening. Leave a foot of the shuttle cord hanging out to the side. Turn the cards another quarter turn away from you. Holes B and C will be on top. Remember to slide the cards back and forth after rotating them in order to open up the split in the warp. Again, firmly pull this opening apart and pass the shuttle through. From now on, pull the weft (the cord on the shuttle) tightly across the warp after each pass of the shuttle. If the weft is too loose, you'll have big floppy loops on the edges of your strap. Turn another quarter turn away. Holes C and D will be on top. Slide the cards, split the warp, and pass the shuttle through. Turn the cards another quarter turn away. Holes D and A will be on top again, with the numbers in the center. You have done a full rotation of the cards. You should begin to see an arrowhead with a light center pointing away from you.

For the next sequence, turn the cards *toward* you. If you always turn the cards away from you, the warp cords would get so twisted that you couldn't rotate the cards. (With the cord we have used, we can do about sixteen quarter turns, or four full card rotations in one direction or the other before we have to turn the other way.) The next four quarter turns toward you will give you another arrowhead pointing in the opposite direction of the one you just completed. Together they will look like a large X. In this pattern, this is the way you get Xs.

If you want two arrowheads pointing the same direction, then turn the cards eight quarter turns away from you when you start. If you want diamonds, begin the weave with four quarter turns toward you, then do four quarter turns away from you. (This is two arrowheads with their base ends connected.) These aren't your only choices with this pattern. You can rotate the cards 5 or 6 or however many times you want in any one direction, and then reverse as many times in the opposite direction as you want. If you don't care about a sequential pattern, then you don't need to keep track of your turns forward or back. You can randomly turn the cards and do all the experimenting you want. Just remember to reverse them once in a while so the warps don't tangle.

The other side of the strap is also forming a pattern, sometimes more intriguing than the one you are watching develop. Remember, since the warp knot is tied to your belt, you will have to adjust the warp on your belt to keep the cards in easy reach. As the woven strap gets longer, the cards get farther away. Untie the warp from your belt and retie into the woven strap when the cards are hard to reach.

As you near the far end of the warp, you will run out of room to rotate the cards. When this happens, you are finished. Untie the upper knot and remove the cards. You can braid or sew the ends or leave them as they are. Your strap is ready to use.

Rope, cord, and string are endlessly useful in hundreds of situations. How satisfying and fun it is to make your own from natural materials. When you've invested yourself into such a project, you'll be surprised how much value even the most basic objects will have.

CHAPTER

III

TOOLS

THE STONE AGE TOOLBOX IS REMARKABLY SIMILAR to what Joe next door has in his red metal Craftsman box in the garage: sanders, polishers, sharpeners, hammers, cutters, planers, groovers, wedges, drills, and awls. The tools described in this chapter may look a little different from Joe's set, but they work just as well and have stood the test of time.

This chapter gives directions for making tools that will be useful in completing the projects throughout this book. These Stone Age tools are made from sticks, stones, bones, antlers, plants, and leather. They are very economical to make and can be easily replaced. Follow the plans in this chapter to fill your Stone Age toolbox step by step.

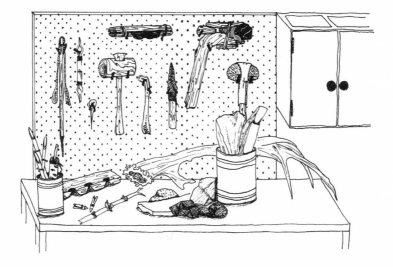

FIRE

Fire is the first tool. Recognizing fire as a tool means you can come up with solutions such as burning a log in half; burning off ends of a log; hollowing out wooden bowls, spoons, or even canoes; firing pottery; smoking hides for water repellency; bending and shaping wood with heat; melting pitch for glue; cooking food; warming houses; and tempering stone to make the task of breaking it into other tools easier. Put your friction fire set in the toolbox.

SANDERS AND POLISHERS

Next, add some sanders and polishers. Rough stones of varying coarseness work very well for sanding, as does sand itself, rubbed on with a piece of leather. The segmented horsetail fern, also called scouring rush (pictured right), contains silicon. Old plants make terrific sanders, and young plants are handy polishers.

Polishers can also be smooth stones or bones. You can burnish wood or clay with polishers. Some sanders and polishers should have flattish surfaces so you can grind objects back and forth against them. Others should be rounded and handheld for getting into small places. Rough sanders make good abraders as well. Abrading wood gives more sticking surface for glue. Abraders are also used in more precise stoneworking. (More on this at the end of the chapter.) Streambeds are logical places to look for polishers, while open hillsides often have flattish sander rocks. However all these tools can be found just about anywhere.

HAMMER

Stones also make excellent hammers, and what toolbox is complete without a hammer? Hammer stones can be handheld or mounted on a wooden handle by pecking a groove around the center girth of the stone and lashing it with cord or rawhide lacing.

Hardwood makes a good hammer as well. This can be as simple as a stout, straight stick about 1 to 2 feet long. A piece of wood with a right-angle bend from where a branch diverged can make a good hammer too. The heftier end should be cut 4 to 6 inches from the bend. If it is much longer, it becomes unstable. Make up a hammer and add it to the toolbox.

SHARP EDGES

Next you'll need some sharp edges. Cutting, scoring, grooving, and chopping can all be done with a sharp-edged rock. If you can't *find* sharp edges, you can make some. (Right now is the time to put on some safety goggles. Buy a pair; these aren't easy to make by primitive methods. Store them in an old sock or rag to prevent them from getting scratched.) Hold a weighty rock above your head and hurl it down to the ground on top of another rock. This should produce some sharp tools. You can also find large, sharp-edged rocks weighing about 5 to 10 pounds and make them into two-handed choppers. The sharp edges combined with the mass make cutting green wood easy. However, the more-curved side of the chopper must face you, while the flatter side must face the wood, allowing the edge to bite into the wood. We've used these two-handed choppers for making drum hoops and bow staves as well as for felling trees. With stone tools, it is important to do your major wood removal while the wood is green. Once wood dries, it becomes harder to work and will dull and chip your tools.

The next step in creating stone tools is predictable tool production called **flintknapping.** This begins by learning to sharpen the edges of your randomly broken or found tools. You will find sharpening directions at the end of this chapter, along with other beginning instructions for flintknapping. But before we dismiss the random sharp edges you have made from smashing rocks or finding them as they are, let's talk about mounting them onto handles. This is called **hafting.** Hafting can be unnecessary if the sharp-edged pieces are large enough to allow a good grip. Adding a handle provides leverage and comfort.

PLANERS

Planers can be made without difficulty. You will need a rock, a stick, a hammer stone, and some lashing. Take a green stick about 1 inch in diameter and 6 inches long. Split it lengthwise by using the sharp-edged rock you are planning to haft and a hammer stone to start it into the stick. Carve out a middle area in the inside of each half of the stick to conform to the contours of the rock piece you are hafting. Use that rock to carve the contour.

Now put the split sides of the stick back together and lash one end tightly with cord or rawhide lacing. Place the rock into the contour so the sharp

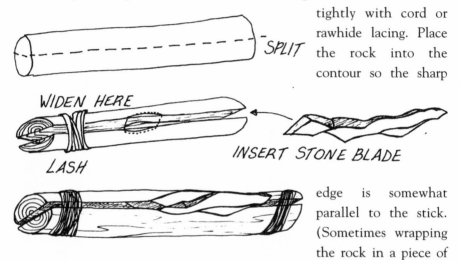

edge is somewhat parallel to the stick. (Sometimes wrapping the rock in a piece of leather first helps give a tighter fit.) Pinch the unlashed ends of the sticks together tightly and lash them securely with half hitches that can be easily untied. This makes replacing the sharp edge quick and easy.

KNIFE

You can haft a sharp rock piece for a knife as well. You need a rock, a stick, cord or rawhide lashing, your abrader and hammer stone, and pitch for glue.

Choose a rock that is thin and about 3 inches long. If you can't *find* a suitable rock, you can make a knife blade by banging a thin slab of rock off a larger rock. (See more details at the end of the chapter.) Using your abrader, dull any sharp edges around the handle area where the lashing will be by grinding those edges until they break off flat.

Then make a handle by cutting a notch about 1 inch deep into the stick with the rock you are about to haft. The notch should be a bit loose so you can adjust the rock to be straight in the handle. If carving into the top of the stick is a problem, split the stick in half lengthwise with the rock you are hafting and a hammer stone. Carve the contours on both sides of the stick and then place the stick back together and lash the handle securely.

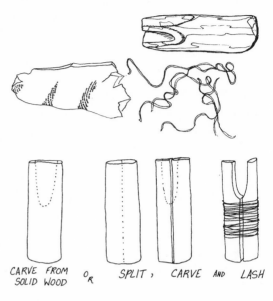

CARVE FROM SOLID WOOD OR SPLIT, CARVE AND LASH

Heat some pitch (see Chapter 10 on glue) and dip the notch in the pitch.

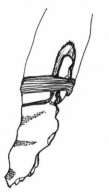

Quickly insert the rock knife in the pitch-filled notch. Move the knife in the desired position and hold until the pitch solidifies. When the pitch cools, scrape off the excess with your fingernails and reinforce the pitch with wet lashing or other cord dipped in hide glue. If the pitch cools before the rock is in the desired position, hold the rock over a heat source and get it hot. The hot rock will melt the pitch and allow you to reposition.

WEDGES AND CLAMPS

You've added a lot of things to your toolbox but you still need a set of wedges. You will need antler or wood and your cutters, grinders, carvers, and groovers. Antler and wood make the most durable wedges. For antler wedges, cut off the tines, the pointed ends, and grind them on two sides to make your wedges for splitting wood. Another good section of antler for wedges is the base of the fork of the tines. This wide part of the antler has a higher portion of outer antler and less spongy center. Make the tapers on the front edges of

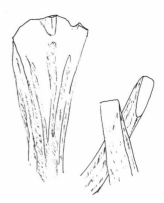

the wedges narrow so they won't have a tendency to pop out when you try to start them into the wood.

Seasoned hardwood also makes good wedges. After grinding and/or chopping and carving the wood to shape, fire harden the tips of the wedges by burying them under coals long enough to bake the wood hard but not burn any part of the wood.

When you start grooving and cutting that antler to make a wedge, you are really going to be wishing for a vice or clamp. You'll need a cord rope, a tree or sturdy fixed pole, a wood wedge, a hammer, and a stout hardwood stick.

The first vice to try is simply a rope-sized cord tied around a tree and the item you want held securely. You can use a pole or a stick in the ground instead of a tree. Tie the cord loosely around both objects. Then insert a stout stick under the cord and twist it tightly like a tourniquet. When you have enough tension to securely hold the object against the tree, tie the end of the stick to the tree with a piece of cord to keep it from untwisting.

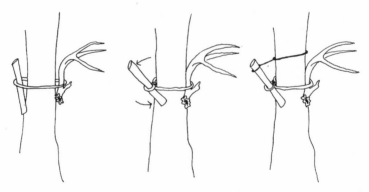

This method can also be used to clamp things to themselves, such as drum hoops, while they are drying. Some cord ropes will not hold up under this kind of twisting. Instead, you can tie the object snugly to the tree or pole; then tap a wedge between the tree and the object you want held securely. (If you haven't made the wedges yet, use a piece of rock and tap it in with one of your hammers.)

For this next simple clamp, you need a stout stick, a cutter, lashing, and a wood wedge or a rock. Take a stout split stick, just like when you hafted the

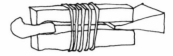

planer, but make your inner contours at the ends of the sticks instead of in the middle. Lash the two halves of the stick together very loosely at the center. Put what you want clamped between the carved-out contours on the one end and tap a wood wedge between the two splits on the other end.

DRILLS

No tool kit would be complete without drills. To make drills, you'll need your bow-drill or hand-drill fire set, a sharp rock edge, and some sand. Use your sharp edge to gouge an indentation where you want to begin drilling. Sprinkle in some sand and start drilling with your fire-drill set. You will need to continue adding sand; the drill will wear down, but so will the surface you are drilling.

Optionally, you can twist a sharp-pointed piece of rock to auger out a hole. You may want to use a piece like this in combination with your fire-drill set. You can chip a stone drill bit and haft it to the drill of your fire set. To make this drill bit, see the end of this chapter. A long, thin bit works best on a hand drill. A chunky, pointed rock works best on a bow drill.

WOODEN MALLET

Once you have a drill, it is easy to make a wooden mallet. It's another type of hammer with endless uses, not the least of which is a croquet mallet. We use ours for cracking acorn shells. You'll need hardwood, a drill, choppers and carvers, sanders, and some fire.

Select a 3-inch or larger hardwood limb for the mallet head, and drill a 1-inch hole clear through its side. Once the hole is drilled, you can burn off the ends until it is about 2 inches from the desired final length. Chop and carve the ends flat. Into the drilled hole of the mallet head, insert a tapered handle that you have chopped, carved, and sanded into shape. Insert the narrow end of the handle into the top of the mallet head. Push the head up

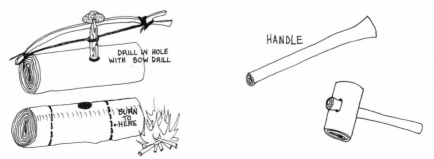

the widening handle until it binds and won't go any further. This tapering handle will tighten in the hole as you use the mallet.

AWLS

Bone, sharp stone, and sanders are needed for a bone awl. Bone awls should be made from sturdy bones that have thick walls such as leg bones.

Score a lengthwise groove in the bone on each side with a sharp piece of rock. This groove will help keep the rock from slipping around too much initially. Make the score in the depression on each side where the leg tendon was lying against the bone.

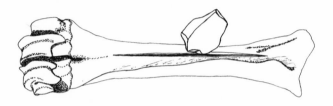

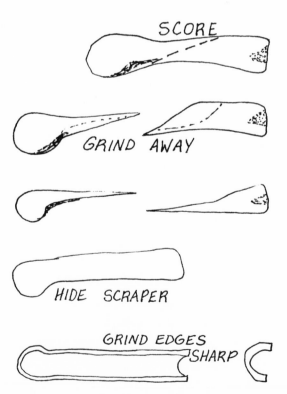

SCORE

GRIND AWAY

HIDE SCRAPER

GRIND EDGES

SHARP

When each side is scored almost through, wedge the rock piece into the end of the bone to split the bone down lengthwise. The bone will split along the grooves you scored. Clean out the marrow, and score another diagonal line in one half of the split bone. Score through the thickness of the bone half. Gently break along the score and you have two bone awls. Grind the pointy ends to needle sharpness starting with a coarse sander and finishing with a smooth one.

Set the other half of the bone aside to make a hide scraping tool. Grind the edges sharp.

BLOW TUBE

In some instances, you will want to be able to enhance the speed of fire as a tool by using a blow tube. A blow tube directs the air to a focused area. This is a handy tool for burning out bowls and spoons. You'll need a hollow stalk and a cutting edge.

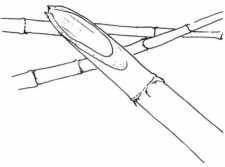

Find a hollow stalk that has a 1/4- to 1/2-inch opening, and cut it in a foot-long section. (This length helps keep smoke out of your face.) For jointed stalks, cut above and below those joints in the section you want to use. Some examples of plants with hollow stalks that work would be teasel, sunflower, and thick grasses. Be careful not to use poisonous plants! If inner pith or joint nodes clog the tube, ream it out with a thin stick carved for this purpose. Take care of this tool; it crushes easily. You can also use this tool to coax a hesitant fire or burn a seat into a wood handle for a hafted axe.

POTTERY TOOLS

A few specialty tools will round out your toolbox and help you complete projects in this book.

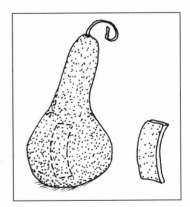

Gourd pieces for shaping and smoothing pottery are quick and easy to make. Cut a curved section of gourd about 2 inches long and 1 inch wide for smaller pots or 2 by 4 inches for larger pots. This tool is handy for scraping the curved walls of the pot to give it a smooth surface. You can also use it to erase your finger marks and press the gritty temper into the clay for a smooth finish. Wet buckskin scraps are also good for smoothing pottery.

Corncobs or cord wrapped around a flat stick help to press texture into the outside surface of cooking pots, which increases surface area and speeds the heating process. This textured surface also makes holding onto the pots easier.

A few other pottery tools that are helpful are sharp sticks to carve designs, brushes of chewed wood and yucca leaves for painting slip designs onto the surface, smooth stones for burnishing, and coarse stones for sanding.

SHUTTLES

Shuttles for netting and weaving are important. The most difficult but also the most beautiful
shuttle we have made came from
the split leg bone of an elk. An
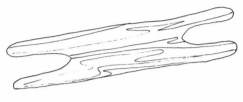
easy wood shuttle can be made quickly, using this diagram as a model.

One of our favorite shuttles, given to us by Steve Edelholm, is simple to make and holds the cord even when hanging down. You'll need a green stick, sinew or thin lashing, hide glue, and two spreader sticks.

To make this shuttle, prepare a green stick 3/8 inch in diameter and 8 inches long. Peel off the bark and wrap it with wet sinew, soaked in hide glue, 2 inches from each end. Let the sinew dry. Then, using a sharp blade, care-
fully split the ends in toward the sinew. Place a spreader stick 1/2 inch in diameter between each of these splits. Form the ends around the spreaders and lash the last 1/2 inch of the sticks back together. This bends the splits into an oval opening. Let it dry a few days. Then remove the end lashings and the spreader sticks.

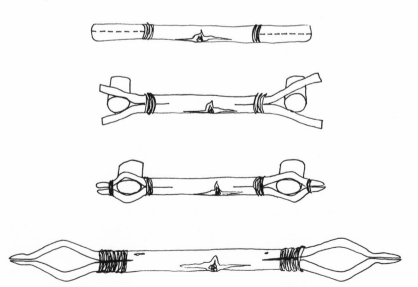

LEATHER TANNING TOOLS

Your last set of specialty tools will be for tanning leather. To make a **beam** on which to flesh and dehair hides, find a smooth log that has a knot-free length and no drying cracks. The log should be about 10 inches in diameter and 6 feet long. Only one section of the log needs this smooth surface—the upper 2 feet where you will be draping the hide for scraping.

Using wedges and a hammer, split the log in half and then burn and chop the ends to 20-degree angles. The top needs to lean against a tree without wobbling, and the bottom needs to dig into the ground instead of sliding toward you. Scrape and sand the working surface smooth; any bumps or

irregularities in the log may cause your scraper to press harder on the hide at that place and cut through.

A **fleshing and dehairing scraper** can be made out of the split leg bone you set aside when making awls. You can also use sharpened rib bones. Whichever you choose, grind the edge to about 60 degrees. You can use a sharp chip of stone and then finish up with a smooth abrading stone.

In the second method of dehairing that we describe in Chapter 9 on animals, your scraper will take a different form. This is actually a **modified clamp scraper.** You will need a stout bent stick, a sharp rock edge, a piece of leather, two shims of wood, and rawhide lashing.

Measure the shorter length of your bent stick and split a second stick that is this same length. Loosely lash the first piece of the split on top of the bent stick, near the bend. Carve the second piece shorter and into a wedge shape.

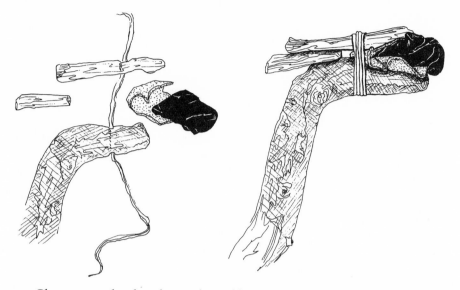

Choose a rock edge that is free of burrs and has a slight curve on the scraping edge. Actually, if you journey into more advanced stoneworking, perfectly shaped rock flakes will be a natural byproduct of your efforts. You may need to wrap the rock with a leather piece to get a good fit. When you insert the rock between the lashing of the first split piece and the bent stick, tap the wedge in to tighten the rock in place.

Hold the scraper with one hand over the top of the bend and one hand on the lower handle. This will give a controlled scraping motion.

To make a **metal-bladed hide scraper,** you'll need a wood or antler handle piece, a metal blade, lashing, and a grinding wheel to bevel the metal edge.

Acquire a junk metal file (available at used-tool stores for a buck) and snap off a 2-inch section. Do this by placing the file on the sidewalk and putting something underneath one end of it, such as another file. Then hit the file where you want to break it with a rock or hammer, making sure your head is turned. Pieces will go flying, but the file should snap where you want it to.

Use a grinding wheel (that same used-tool store often has a hand-crank model for under $10) to round the front cutting edge of the metal blade. Then bevel the last 1/2 inch at a 20-degree angle. Unless you do all this grinding slowly on the grinder and immerse the blade in water often so it doesn't get too hot, the metal will lose its temper and the blade will dull easily while you are scraping. After the 20-degree edge is achieved, finish grinding the last 1/16 inch off at a 45-degree angle. This angle is adequately sharp for dehairing and will hold its edge well. The first grind to 20 degrees is for thinning the blade so you don't have to remove so much metal each time you sharpen it.

Make a notch in the side of your handle just large enough to accept the back end of your metal blade. The blade should stick out of the handle at about a 95-degree angle. This angle will allow more control when scraping so the blade won't dig in too deeply, cutting the hide. Use wet rawhide to secure the blade to the handle.

In the second dehairing method, you will also find a **frame** useful. Take poles at least 3 inches in diameter and notch the ends like the Lincoln Log toys. Set the poles in a square and lash each corner securely with thick rawhide or heavy cord. Then notch and lash corner supports to keep the frame from warping as the hide dries and puts tension on the frame. (You can alternatively use nails and scrap lumber. Just make sure it is at least 2" x 4" lumber to prevent warping.)

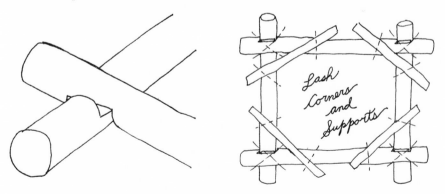

The last thing you need for tanning hides is a set of about 40 twig clips. These clips hold the hide in a closed bag shape when smoking it for water repellency.

Break off green twigs about 1 1/4 inches long with a bud knot on each twig. Use a sharp chip to split the twig to the knot. The knot will keep it from splitting all the way. Use these clips like old-fashioned clothespins.

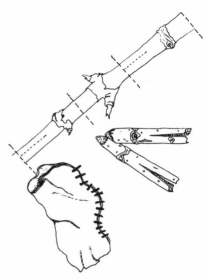

Your toolbox is loaded by now and probably overflowing. Next time your friends come over and the inevitable bragging about the power tools begins, you can take out your 10-pound two-hand chopper and watch them back up a pace! You've accumulated a lot of useful and attractive Stone Age tools. If you are still interested in predictable stoneworking, read on.

FLINTKNAPPING

Stoneworking to get a planned tool is a lot like doing a puzzle, but instead of adding pieces together to come up with a final solution, you take pieces away to achieve the final tool shape. The art of predictable stone-tool working is called **flintknapping.**

Our ancestors probably moved from the stick-and-bone age into the Stone Age by first randomly breaking rocks and then learning to sharpen the edges of their dulled tools. Let's re-create this historical journey by learning to sharpen the edge of your found or randomly created two-handed chopper. The first thing to remember is that for heavy use, a thirty- to sixty-degree edge is just fine, so don't try to sharpen your chopper edge to a steel-knife thinness. A stone edge with any sharper angle may crumble during chopping.

Before you sharpen, you need to have a good hammer stone. Gritty rocks that are soft but resist crumbling make good hammer stones. The grit grips the rock you are chipping, giving good purchase instead of glancing off when striking. You want a softer rock because it will absorb some of the energy, reducing the shock in your chopper and making the stone peel off in longer sections. A good hammer stone can create a better edge on your chopper and will be helpful later on when you start making tools out of these pieces you chip off. So pick strong sandstone or limestone as opposed to granite, quartzite, or basalt. In a pinch, use any roundish stone you find that fits easily in your hand. Look in streambeds for these. Be sure to dry them a bit before using, as wet rock crumbles more easily than dry.

To sharpen a chopper edge, put on your safety goggles. Place the chopper on the ground or on your leg protected by a heavy pad of leather. Tilt the chopper so the edge you are going to hit is supported by your leg or the ground. This support keeps the edge from crumbling under the force of the blow and allows that force to move through the stone, peeling off thin sections of stone, called flakes, and leaving a sharper edge on your chopper.

Look at the angles and dimensions in figures 1 and 2. Note the outward arc of the blow force. Strike the chopper edge just this way along the entire cutting edge, removing successive flakes. By keeping the proper angle, you will have sharpened your chopper.

Fig. 1

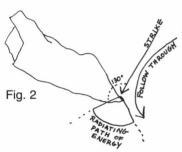

Fig. 2

Now let's look at the how's and why's of what you have done. When most folks want to break a rock, their tendency is to hit it straight on or hit into the rock to chip out flakes. The reason to hit the stone at the *angle* described is because of the way energy travels. It generally travels in a predictable pattern. For an example, think of a BB hitting a pane of glass. A tiny cone of glass will often pop out on the inside of the pane. The force of a blow moves outward from the point of impact in a widening cone.

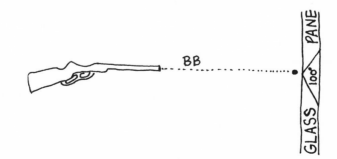

Figure 2 shows the force of your blow and its cone pattern to take off a sharpening flake from the edge of your chopper. Most of the cone goes out into the air and the flake breaks off along the edge of the cone. This is exactly what you want for getting thin flakes. Figure 3 shows the force of your blow when you strike more directly into the rock. For taking flakes, this angle is unsuitable, but for splitting the rock in half, it works. Figure 4 shows how a straight-on blow merely crushes the edge you want to sharpen. The cone edge where the break would be isn't even on the rock!

Think again about that BB example. It's helpful to look at the angles of a cone formed this way because so many rocks contain high amounts of silicon that the way they break is often similar to the way glass breaks. Working with these approximate angles allows you to move from the random and haphazard to the predictable. The angle of the BB cone on a pane of glass is about 100 degrees. The cone angle in figures 2, 3, and 4 is also about 100 degrees. If you measure the angle from the line of your blow to the break in the stone (or the path of the BB to the edge of its resulting cone), it will be about 130 degrees. Knowing this allows you to decide where to strike and to predict where the break in the rock will be.

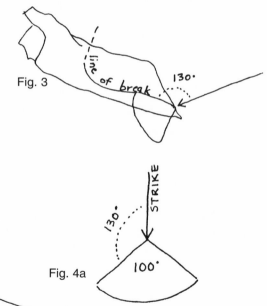

On the previous page we emphasized striking in an outward arc not only helps keep the line of your strike and the break line at the correct angle but gives a clean, prying motion to your blow. If you don't arc your swing away like figure2, you'll often get results like figure 3, or worse, figure 4.

As you strike the rock and successfully peel off flakes, you will begin to notice that many of the flakes have a similar shape. They are curved like the side of a bell. Not only does the energy move out like a cone, but it also moves along the edges of that cone in waves like the ripples on a pond. The first waves or ripples are the largest. The more force used to break off the flake, the larger will be its initial wave or curve. Over time, you will learn that striking with more or less force and using a softer or harder hammer, as well as the density and outside shape of the stone itself, will all produce greater or lesser curves in the flakes. You can use different tools or different forces to get the shape of curve and length of break you want (figure5).

Fig. 5

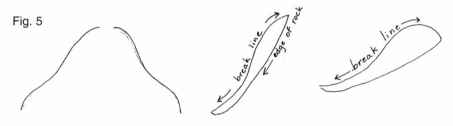

Figuring angles. The reason we've wanted to tell you some hows and whys of the way the breaking happens is because we have this nifty little aid for determining where to strike on your stone, at what angle to strike, and where you can expect the break line to be. To use this aid, you needed to see the conelike radiation of your strike force, get the sense of that cone angle being 100 degrees, see the approximate strike line and resulting break-line angle along the edge of the cone being 130 degrees, and recognize the predictable wave or bell shape of the break. Got that? OK.

Here's the aid: a cardboard cone. Cut a shape out of cardboard like this drawing. (Even though it is one-dimensional, you need to imagine it having complete dimension, like a cone.) Don't worry if the angles aren't *exact* (figure 6).

Right-handed knappers will hold the rock in their left hand and the hammer stone in the right. When using the cardboard cone, hold the stone as you would if breaking it. Hold the cardboard cone

Fig. 6

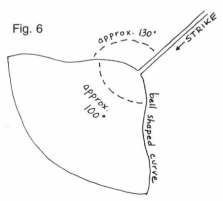

with your right hand, using the left side of the cone as a guide for where the break line would be. It is the opposite for a left-handed knapper: the right side of the cone would be the break line.

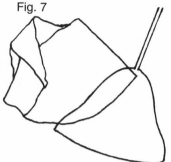

Fig. 7

Hold this cardboard cone on your rock chunk at random spots. Move it here and there, each time choosing a strike-force line and then looking where the resulting break would be. Is the break line out in space? Well that won't work. Is it right in the middle of the rock? If you're trying to get a flake, that's not what you want. Adjust until the break line is where you want it, close along the edge of the rock, with most of the 100-degree cone radiating into air space (figure 7).

So, you've played around with your cone shape and rock a little bit. Now give it a whack with the hammer stone and see what happens. Remember to support the rock against your leg or the ground. Choose some of the same lines you did with the cardboard cone. Don't forget to arc your strike away from the rock.

The 90-degree rule. Did you notice that if you chose to strike on rock edges with angles greater than 90 degrees your hammer stone just bounced away without biting in and removing a flake? "No fair!" You probably yelled. "My strike angle and break line were at the right places!" Yes, that's true. But that greater-than-90-degree angle in the rock you wanted to break stopped you. When you're trying to strike on a rock angle greater than 90 degrees, even if the break line looks like it will go in the right place, your strike angle becomes so shallow and indirect that it does not deliver the necessary force. The hammer stone merely bounces off. So, when examining the rock to plan your strike-and-break strategy for taking off flakes, always choose rock angles that are less than 90 degrees. Remember, as in figure 3, if you actually want to break your rocks in half—and you may want to do this to give your rock

Fig. 8

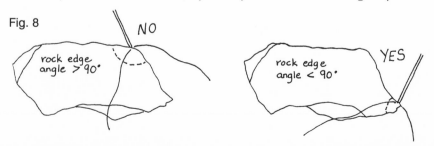

NO

rock edge
angle >90°

rock edge
angle < 90°

YES

more favorable angles, setting it up for taking off flakes—go ahead and hit the rock accordingly.

Making flake tools. Now you know enough of the hows and whys to pick up a rock and make a chopper in a predictable way. This allows you to also make flake tools—knife blades, scrapers, or planers—that are beyond random breaking. You may also find some of the flakes are the perfect shape for hide scrapers. These will have a curved, unburred end similar to the metal hide scraper you learned earlier how to make from a file. Save these flakes so you'll have plenty for dehairing method number 2.

Take a lot of time to practice breaking rocks. Don't be frustrated if your first attempts don't produce desirable results. It might not be your technique; some rocks just work better than others. However, you don't have to take the journey to El Dorado to find workable rocks. Something that will work for you can be found in almost every geographic region. In fact, one of our favorite games at home is to lay out a variety of stone tools and guess where the stones have come from. By the time we're finished, almost every area in the country has been represented. If your busting and breaking forays aren't panning out, contact your local university and talk to people in the geology or archaeology departments or call your local rock shop for help in locating good rock deposits.

Up to this point, you've learned how to make and sharpen the edge of a chopper with a hammer stone, and you've learned how to take flakes off larger rocks. These flakes, as we've said, are tools in their own right. When these flake tools become dull, you'll want to sharpen them. All the previous principles apply, but now you're working on a smaller scale. Hold the flake tool that needs sharpening in your hand. Having some scrap leather to protect your hand will often be necessary.

To remove large chips for a sharp edge, gently tap the dulled edge with a small hammer stone. To remove longer chips, a hammer made out of the large, rounded base of an antler will often work better.

Squeezing the bottom of the stone for support where the chip will peel off will also increase length. Use your fingers for support. If the edge breaks off sharp but it's the wrong shape, you may still want to remove more stone to get the shape you need. You'll need to grind, or abrade, the edge with a rough rock before striking. The hammer stone will work for this. Abrading thickens and strengthens the edge. Otherwise, the edge may crumble with the blow. Abrading is not usually necessary when sharpening tools that have been used, as the edges are sufficiently dulled through use and therefore strengthened.

For fine work, or with thin-flake tools, you will need either an antler tine or a piece of copper grounding wire mounted in a wooden handle to press off chips. These tools are called **pressure flakers.** The small chips are removed by slow pressure instead of striking with a rock or antler hammer.

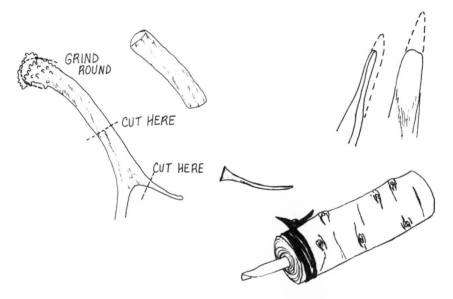

A good length for pressure flakers is 4 or 5 inches. Copper grounding wire is available at hardware stores. Get the largest size. Cut off 1-1/2 inches of this wire. Drill a hole slightly smaller than the wire 1 inch deep in a 1-inch-diameter stick. Pound the wire into this hole. Then harden the wire and shape it at the same time by hitting it several times between a hammer and the sidewalk or between two rocks. The two most usable point shapes for us have been round and flat (like a flat-head screwdriver). The round tip is for heavy pressure, and the screwdriver tip is for getting into spots where the other tip is too wide. Antler tines work well but get dull quickly and have to be sharpened periodically. Use whatever you can get hold of.

To press off chips, first dull the edge you want to sharpen or shape a little with an abrading stone, if necessary. Place a thick pad of leather underneath the rock to protect your palm from the jab of the tool point when the chip releases. This leather will also support the chip, keeping it from

breaking off short. Then press the
tool into the stone and down. A chip
should come off the bottom edge.

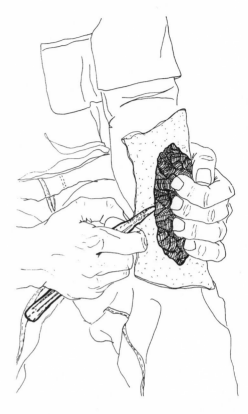

Copper flakers seem to work best
when pressed just above the edge you
are chipping. This is because of the
copper's tendency to crush the edge if
pressed directly into it, especially
with weaker stones such as obsidian.
In contrast, antler flakers will often
slip off if used above the edge. They
usually need to be pressed directly
into the edge to get a grip. If you'll be
using antler to sharpen and shape,
the edge you are working should not
be abraded as much or allowed to get
as dull in use because of the antler's
tendency to slip off and not release
the chip.

Because pressing off long chips is
physically harder than striking them
off with a hammer, and since chips struck off tend to be larger than those
pressed off, experienced flintknappers rely on striking off chips for large stone
removal and thinning. They press off flakes as a last resort, when striking
would break the piece or crush the edge.

Another tip in chip and flake removal is to draw the outline on the stone
where the next flake will detach. (Use a pencil, felt-tip pen, or piece of charcoal.) This will help you get better at predicting how far a flake will run,
which is what flintknapping is about.

Sometimes your chips and flakes will snap off abruptly instead of thinning out to a nice sharp edge at the bottom. This break at the bottom can be
caused by several reasons. The diagrams in series A at the top of page 88
show how this may happen. Breaks such as this are the flintknapper's neme-
sis because they form a wall that successive flakes cannot penetrate. These
walls should be removed before trying to continue further. Removal strategies are shown in figure series B.

Series A Some reasons the flakes may not travel as long as you want them to:

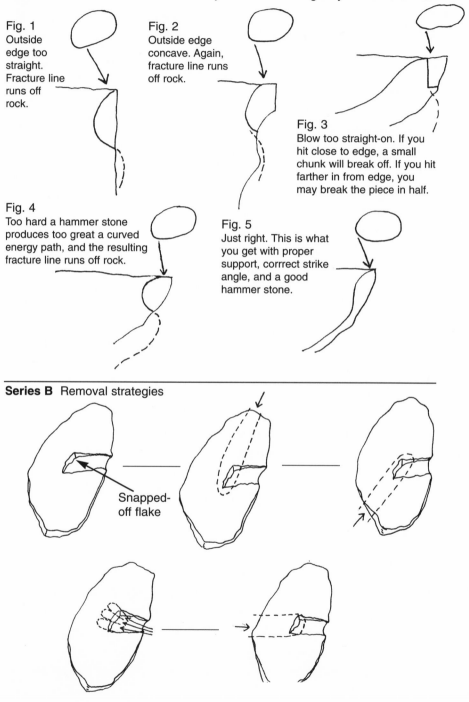

Fig. 1
Outside edge too straight. Fracture line runs off rock.

Fig. 2
Outside edge concave. Again, fracture line runs off rock.

Fig. 3
Blow too straight-on. If you hit close to edge, a small chunk will break off. If you hit farther in from edge, you may break the piece in half.

Fig. 4
Too hard a hammer stone produces too great a curved energy path, and the resulting fracture line runs off rock.

Fig. 5
Just right. This is what you get with proper support, corrrect strike angle, and a good hammer stone.

Series B Removal strategies

Snapped-off flake

DRILL BIT

The last tool to add to the toolbox is a drill. Pressure flaking allows you to form a good drill bit. Make the bit from a stone flake and chip it into the shape.

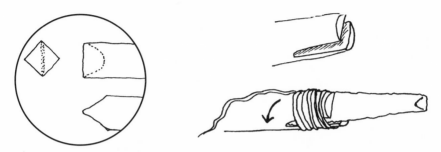

For thin bits, haft the bit to a hand drill with hot pitch and sinew. If you haft a small-diameter bit to a bow drill and drill deeply, you will often snap the bit in two, as the bit binds. Even with a hand drill, it is still possible to snap the bit, especially if you tilt the drill or drill deep and bind. A leather thong (see below) attached at the top with thumb loops 6 inches down will keep you drilling straight, preventing that cause of

bit snapping. If the bit binds because you are drilling deep, stop and ream out the hole with a handheld bit of larger diameter. Then you can continue drilling deeper with the hand drill without binding or breaking the bit.

As you are starting to imagine, flintknapping is a big subject capable of occupying and consuming the minds of those for a proclivity and weakness toward physics and mechanical engineering. But in justification, it could be considered at the heart of the Stone Age.

As a species, because of the tools we have made, our bodies have changed. Stones, and now steel, have largely taken the place of sharp teeth and claws; machines have taken the place of muscles. Tools have allowed us to take a radically different evolutionary path than the animals with which we share the world. And it all began with a randomly broken edge of stone. So lift that rock high and hurl it down. Enjoy the journey.

CHAPTER IIII

COLOR

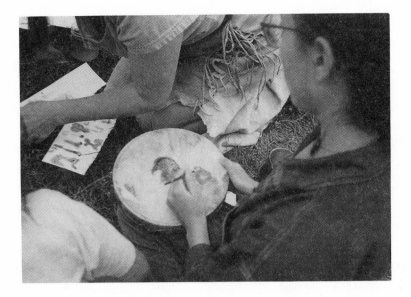

THE HUES OF THE RAINBOW ARE SCATTERED around your neighborhood or closely surrounding area. Many different kinds of common, easily identifiable plants, as well as soils, can be transformed into lovely dyes, stains, and paints with very little effort.

EARTH PIGMENTS

Let's look at paints first. Natural paints are everywhere. The first place to search is on the ground. Watch for claylike soils that have strong color already. Red, yellow, gray, or white clay soils are the most common. You can simply rub the earth right onto the material you want to color, but to make paint you need to first separate the pigment from the soil by a settling process.

Here's how: Dig some of the soil. Spread it out and let it dry. Crush it to a powder using a *mano* and *metate*, which can be as simple as a cinder block against the sidewalk or two specially chosen rocks. Mix the soil with water (about one part soil to two parts water) and let it settle for a few hours. (Just go away and do something else. It will do what it's supposed to do.) When you come

back, pour off the clear water layer on top of the pigment. The next layer is a small viscous layer of color above the coarse soil. Carefully pour this layer onto a tray or bowl. This is your usable pigment. The remaining soil can be dried, crushed again, and the settling process repeated.

This earth pigment can be used in many different ways. Your first option is to paint something; rub the pigment on arrow shafts or whatever.

The next option is to let the pigment dry. Just leave it in the tray you poured it onto and put it in the sun or place it in a low oven, food dehydrator, or under a heat lamp. Once it has dried, you can crush it into powder and store it indefinitely, or you can roast the pigment to change the resulting paint color. (Use a flat rock by the fire, or a cast-iron skillet.) Different roasting times and temperatures give different degrees of color, or sometimes different colors altogether. This is really fun to experiment with. When you are ready to paint something, either reconstitute with water or make a base or fixative for the pigment with oil, fat, plant extract, hide glue, or egg.

Charcoal makes a great black paint. Don't use briquettes! They are gross. Use burnt organic matter. Grind it to a powder and add it to bases, just like soil pigment.

PIGMENT BASE

To make a plant-extract pigment base or fixative, try this: Chop up some prickly pear cactus pads and boil with water until the liquid is thicker than water. Strain off the plant pieces and add the pigment to this base. Mix well. You're ready to paint! This works well when you want the paint to be water resistant, for example, on wooden objects, rawhide containers, rattles, etc., that will be exposed to moisture.

If you use oil, fat, egg white, or hide glue as a base, you don't need to cook anything down; just mix in the pigment and use the resulting paint. Oil and fat work great for face paints (kids love this) or hard leather work. Egg white and hide glue work well on wood, rawhide, clay, or plant fiber. They are not as waterproof as prickly pear and should be waterproofed if the items will be exposed to moisture. Pitch varnish, described in Chapter 10 on glue, makes a great cover for painted objects too.

Store your paints in the dried, powdered-pigment form rather than in the bases. Except when mixed with oil or rendered fat, they just don't keep well or work as well as when they are made up fresh.

PLANT PIGMENTS

Bee plant makes a wonderful pigment for pottery decoration. Paint your designs on before firing the pots, and the outcome can be designs in white, black, blue, or iridescent purple, depending on the heat and amount of oxygen in the pottery firing. The results are not always predictable, so the outcome is a fun surprise. Just boil the beeplant in water (leaves, stalk, and flower) for an hour. Remove the plant matter and continue to cook the liquid until it is like syrup. Paint this syrup on the greenware pottery. Freeze the rest of the beeplant syrup or dry it to a "leather" (like fruit leather).

Making stains from fruit is easy. Mash up berries and apply them to the object you want to stain. Blackberry, raspberry, and twinberry stain purple. Strawberry stains pink or red. Chokecherry stains dark brown. Try all kinds and see for yourself what happens.

Dyes are numerous and the possibilities are expansive. We've chosen a few here that are easy to identify and try. Almost anything that stains your hands when you are working with it can be used. One nice thing about dyes is that, should you accidentally stain an article of clothing, you can dye it a darker color and still wear it with pride. You probably will even get pleasant comments from friends about your earthy colored clothing.

Dyes also can add contrast to weavings. We wind up with bushels of buckskin scraps every year. One can only use so many small pouches and hacky sacks. So, we have started cutting those scraps into lacing and using this lacing for netted bags and card weaving. (See Chapter 2.) We dye some of the lacing different colors, and these make pleasing patterns when woven. Remember when dyeing leather or rawhide to keep the water temperature lukewarm or cooler. Also, don't soak the leather much longer than overnight or it could start to rot. Buckskin and rawhide will readily accept dyes, often easier than wool, so you can get away with less soaking time.

Here are some dyes that don't need to be "set" with mordants. Let's start in the kitchen. **Coffee makes a great dye.** Brew it strong and soak your cloth, yarn, rawhide, or buckskin in the cooled brew. How long you soak it will determine the final color. Yellow onion skins make a lovely yellow color. Boil down the skins and soak the material. Again, the amount of soaking time will determine the intensity of the color. Tomato sauce or catsup will dye pink to reddish brown, depending on strength, time, and temperature while dyeing.

Although mordants are not necessary with these dyes, experimenting with them can be fun. They can help get a longer-lasting color and even cause dramatic changes in color shades. Alum is one mordant. It can be scraped up along roadsides throughout the West. Look for areas where water and minerals have evaporated and left behind a crusty white coating on the soil. Throw some in the pot while the dye is being prepared.

Now let's head to the vacant lot or near a stream to round up some more plants for dye.

Larkspur is a common plant and easy to find. It has several blue or purple flowers on its stalk. The upper sepal is a long cone, almost like a cornucopia, that ends with the open flower. It makes a greenish gray dye. Pick the flowers and mix them with enough water to be covered. Set the container in the warm sun. After a day or two mash the flowers and add your yarn or cloth. Leave the container in a warm spot about one week until the dye begins to ferment. During the week, periodically work the material into the dye. Rinse your material well after dyeing.

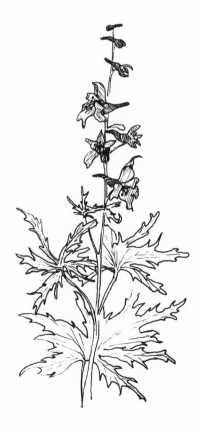

Indian paintbrush (right) makes a greenish yellow dye. Its flowers come in yellow, green, pink, red, and orange. It gets its name because it looks like an old brush dipped in paint. The flowers occur in dense spikes. To make dye, use the same procedure as for larkspur.

Alder trees are common and their bark makes a variety of dye colors. You may get red, orange, or brown. The trees grow in moist areas, often along streams. They look similar to birches and willows with catkins hanging down, but their bark is reddish. Take two pounds bark from the male tree and break it into pieces. Boil the pieces in five gallons of water for two hours. Strain off bark pieces and soak your material overnight. Rinse well. This dye can be stored for later use, as the acid prevents rotting.

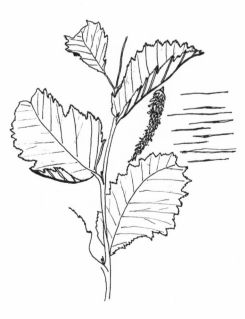

Bee plant makes a great dye too (as well as being edible) and gives a nice yellow green color very different from that of Indian paintbrush. It has pink or yellow flowers that grow in clusters, and pods that look similar to tiny string beans that appear while the plant is still flowering. Fill a large pot with whole bee plants. Add water to cover. Cook the plants until they are very mushy. Mash the plants and remove large stalks. Add your material and set in a warm place for a week. Periodically work the material into the dye. After one week, boil the whole pot of dye and material for a few hours; then set aside another week until the dye begins to ferment. Rinse well.

Juniper makes a yellow tan dye. Boil a pound of twigs and leaves in two gallons of water for an hour. Strain out the twigs and use. Increasing the dyeing time and boiling the dye while the material is in it will increase the color intensity.

Black walnut makes a brown gray dye. Crush and then soak a pound of the hulls for eight hours in two gallons of water. Again, boiling and long soaking times will increase intensity of color.

Soil pigments can also be used as dyes. Mix pigment in water and cover raw wool, yarn, cloth, leather, or rawhide. Your material will soak up the color. Let it sit as long as you want. If you gently cook the pigment with the wool or cloth in the pot (simmer 3–4 hours), the color will increase according to the length of time it is cooked.

These color ideas are fun and easy. With materials as simple as a container, or a container and fire, you are ready to paint, stain, or dye some beautiful hues. Color your world!

CHAPTER

BASKETS
BUCKETS
BOWLS

WE USE BASKETS, BUCKETS, AND BOWLS EVERY DAY in a gamut of imaginative ways. You can create some unique, useful, and outrageously beautiful containers from natural materials that grow abundantly in your area. Tupperware, move over!

GOURD-BOTTOM BAG

Let's start out with a gourd-bottom bag. Netted-top gourd bags are good for storing fruits and vegetables in the kitchen, while a buckskin top makes a great purse. These gourd bottom bags are also ideal for storing dried herbs, teas, and berries and adding storage space to an area where you can hang them from the ceiling. You'll need a gourd, a sharp cutting stone or knife, a drill to make holes in the gourd, buckskin and lacing, and a bone awl. You can optionally use cloth or whatever you have for the top of the gourd container. Any size gourd will do.

The first gourd bag we received from our friend Matt was very small, and we have since made some fairly large ones.

Cut the bottom of the gourd by scoring an even line around it with a sharp edge. Slowly and evenly deepen the score. When the edge begins to cut through the gourd wall, be sure the top and bottom of the gourd are completely free of one another before you try to pull them apart. Save the top part of the gourd for disk rattles, reet reets (see Chapter 11 on music), or for pottery tools (see Chapter 3 on tools).

Gently scrape the inside of the gourd until it is clean. Then drill lacing holes around its top edge, making sure not to drill so close to the edge that the holes split out. A stone drill bit on a hand drill works well for this.

Decide how tall you want the bag to be and cut a piece of buckskin (or cloth) the length you want and with a width that will wrap completely around the gourd, leaving a small overlap to stitch a seam. (See Chapter 2 on rope, string, and thread if you prefer to make a net top or weave cloth from cord. If you want to make a netted top, begin the mesh starting chain on the gourd itself. Prepare lacing or cord for fastening the top material to the gourd bottom and for sewing up the seam.)

Punch holes in the bottom edge of the buckskin with your awl. Have these holes align with the gourd holes. Also punch matching holes up both sides of the buckskin to sew the side seam, and punch a final row of holes in the top edge to lace a drawstring.

Lay the buckskin over the gourd holes. Begin lacing at one side of the buckskin, go all the way around, and continue lacing up the side seam. Tie a knot at the top. Use a separate piece of lacing to run a drawstring through the top edge.

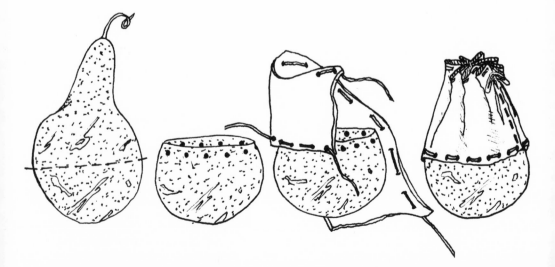

LOG BOWL

You can make log containers by
using a coal to burn out the inside
and then carving and sanding the
outside. You'll need a log, wood or
antler wedges and a wood mallet, a

fire and a pair of grippers to pick up coals, and a blow tube to get started. (See
Chapter 1 on fire and Chapter 3 on tools.)

Start by splitting a log in half lengthwise with the wedge and mallet.

Mark the shape of the container opening on the inner side of one of the
splits.

Place a coal in the center of this marked space and begin blowing
steadily on the coal to burn out the wood. Using a blow tube allows the coal
to burn quickly in a concentrated area.

After a while the char buildup in the deepening container area prevents
the coal from burning into the wood and slows your progress. Dump the coal
back into the fire; then use a sharp stone edge to scrape all the char away
until the wood sides are exposed again. Pick up a new coal and keep going.
Sometimes the sides begin to burn out further than you want them to. You
can wet the bowl in these areas or pack snow around the edges as you work.

When you have burnt out the desired area, dump the coal, wet the bowl,

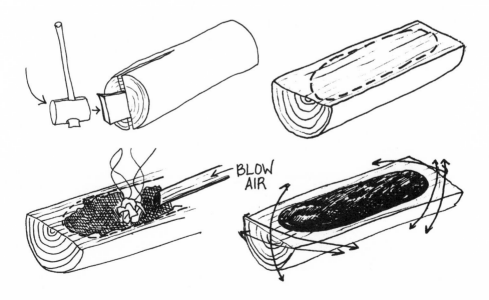

and scrape out all the char. Put sand in the container and rub it vigorously with a scrap of buckskin to smooth the inner walls.

Carve and sand the outside of the log to the desired shape using a hafted one-blow stone tool (see Chapter 3 on tools) and sand in buckskin or a rough sandstone rock. When the bowl is the shape and smoothness that you want it, rub it down well with rendered fat or olive oil. (See Chapter 9 on animals for getting rendered deer and elk fat.)

BARK BUCKET

Carriers made from bark are very attractive and fun to make. You will need bark, a cutting edge, a stone bit drill, lacing material, and flexible twigs or split bark to make a rim.

Begin by cutting a rectangular piece of bark. Smooth barks such as maple, birch, and willow work well, as do more coarse barks such as cedar and juniper. Look for fresh bark from recently felled trees, wind storm casualties, tree trimmers' trash piles, limbs of large trees, or suckers around the bases of trees. These are all abundant options that allow you to collect bark without cutting into the trunk of a tree. (If you take bark from a limb, make sure to only cut on one side of the limb, not all the way around the circumference.) Use a sharp stone edge to cut the rectangular piece of bark and pry up a corner. Be sure your cuts go all the way through the bark to the wood; then gently pull the rectangle away from the limb. Also, be sure that the bark has the same width throughout the piece you cut.

To prevent the bark from drying out while you work with it, leave it soaking in water. Always work gently with the bark, from the initial gathering to the drilling and the final lacing. Roughly handled or dried-out bark will crack and split.

Lay the rectangle of bark with the outer bark down and draw a line across the width of the rectangle at the halfway mark. Then score an eye shape on either side of this midway line. These scores should be deep enough for the bark to bend but not so deep to cut through the entire piece. Make sure the outer edges of the "eye" come very close together so you can bend the edges freely without splitting the bark or leaving wide gaps at the bottom of your container.

Gently fold the two sides of the container up from the scores. Our friend Jeff, who first showed us how to make these containers, puts the bottom eye on his leg as he folds up the sides, in order to support the bottom as it curves up and inward.

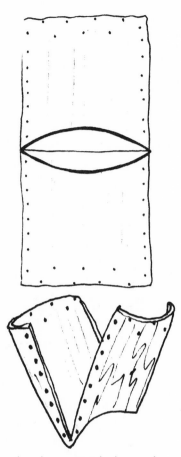

When you know you have a good fold, lay the bark flat again so you can drill holes. You can use the log the bark came from for the drilling surface to help support the bark during drilling and hold it in place. Drill matching holes on both sides of the bark. Keep the holes away from the edges to avoid splits. Along the top edges, drill alternating holes in two rows for lacing on the rim. Make sure these top-edge holes are far enough apart to fit your rim.

When the holes are ready, lace up the sides with cord, bark strips, or buckskin. Place the rim—made from split saplings, bark strips, thick cord, or, for real pizzazz, a card-woven belt (see Chapter 2 on rope)—around the top edge between the alternating holes, and lace diagonally around the top.

If your lacing is long enough, make a handle from the tail ends. We use our bark baskets for acorn gathering, berry picking, and bringing home fresh fish. They make unique mailboxes as well!

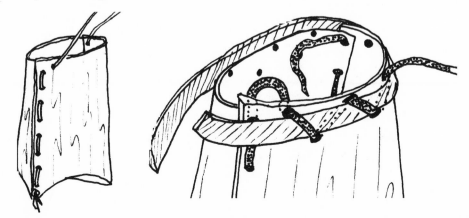

Willow Twine Basket

Making whole-shoot willow twine baskets is fun. There are several different ways to start the weaving.

To make a fish trap, tying the willow ends together in a bundle is a quick-and-easy start that lends to the design of a fish trap.

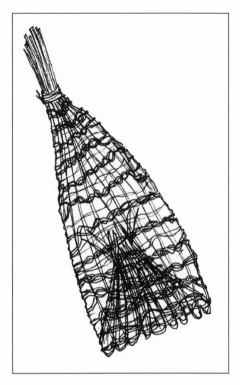

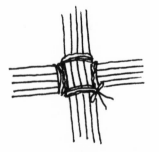

Another quick-and-easy start is tying a cross of willows together with cord. This also works well if you use cord for the basket instead of willows.

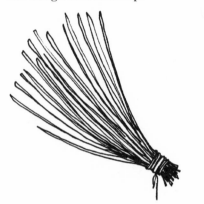

A locked-in cross start, shown to us by Peg Mathewson, is great for making pack baskets, wool-washing baskets, trash cans, laundry hampers, egg-collecting baskets, or any other basket shape or use you want.

You will need lots of straight and flexible willow shoots. (Any other flexible material could be used instead, i.e., weeping willow branches, cloth, yarn, or roots.) The longer they are, the less splicing you have to do. A sharp cutting edge helps so you can sharpen the shoots when you add them as spokes, and a sturdy wooden awl is handy for prying into tightly twined openings when you want to finish the top of the basket or shove in a stubborn spoke shoot.

If you have chosen either of the tied-together basket starts, you can begin twining right away. The two shoots that you start with are called *weavers,* and you will twine them around and around, splicing as they get short. Pick any two shoots next to each other. The other shoots coming out of the start are called *spokes*. Twine the weavers around these. Go right to step 11 and begin twining your weavers.

To begin the locked-cross start, lay 8 willow shoots together in a cross formation with 4 shoots below, the ends pointing east and west, and 4 shoots above, the ends pointing north and south. (We're using these directional words for clarity, so put away your compass!) Since the 8 shoots come together in the middle, they now each have two sets of ends sticking out from that middle. This gives you 16 ends sticking out from the center, 4 in each direction. This looks like the New Mexico sun symbol. (We were theorizing the other day that possibly this sun symbol was originally a basket weaver's petroglyph. You know, one of those old rock signs that meant, "Hey, everybody! Basket Weavers Guild meets next Thursday night. Be there!")

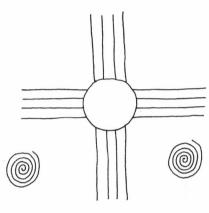

Fourteen of these ends will be the spokes of the basket and 2 of them will be the first weavers.

1. The next nine figures show the willows spaced apart to make it easier for you to see how they are manipulated, but you need to place your willows tightly together. Starting with number 10, the illustrations show the weaving as it would actually be.

2. Hold the cross start before you in your hand. Bend the willow shoot on the right side of the north 4 ends backward, behind, and down around the east 4 ends.

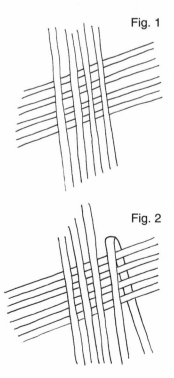

Fig. 1

Fig. 2

3. As it comes around the bottom of the east ends, pull it forward, sharply to the left, and over the front of the south ends.

4. Now place it behind the west ends facing upward so it is once again part of the group of ends pointing north, only now on the left side of the group. This shoot will become one of your two weavers.

5. The topmost willow shoot of the west end becomes your second weaver. Push it back to the right, behind, and around the north ends. This locks the first weaver in place.

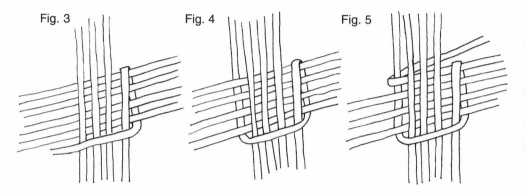

Fig. 3   Fig. 4   Fig. 5

6. Now pull it forward, down, and over the east ends.

7. Bend it sharply to the left around the back of the south ends.

8. Finally, pull it upward and in front of the west ends. The two weavers are now side by side in the northwest corner of the start. Both weaver ends are pointing north.

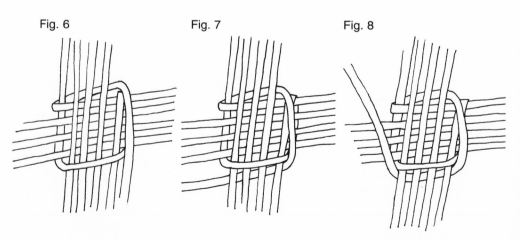

Fig. 6   Fig. 7   Fig. 8

9. To lock in the second weaver, twist the two weaver ends together and begin twining. Push the second weaver end to the right of the first weaver. Pull that first weaver end forward on the outer left side.

10. This is how your start will really look, with all the willows close together. The two weaver shoots look like the top of an **X** now.

11. Push the first north-end spoke into the **X** made by the weavers. The second weaver should be behind the spoke and off toward the right, while the first weaver is off to the left of the spoke and slightly in front.

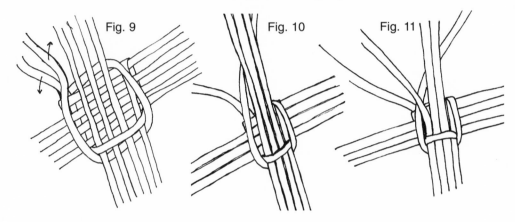

12. Push the first weaver to the right and around in front of the first spoke. Let the end of this first weaver fall back behind the second spoke. Now pull the second weaver forward, over the first weaver, and out in front of the second spoke. You have completed your first twining around a spoke.

13. Continue this exact pattern of twining around each spoke.

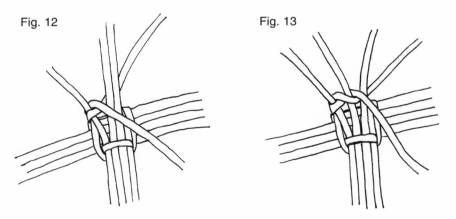

14. Always be sure that the weaver in front gets pushed behind the spoke you are about to twine and is underneath the other weaver as you bring that one forward and in front of the next spoke. This is actually fairly simple to do. You get used to just pushing each spoke into the x of your last twine, and then grab-bing both weavers between your thumb and pointer and giving them a sharp

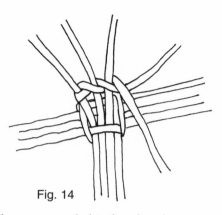

Fig. 14

twist toward you. Your thumb pushes the front weaver behind and under at the same time your pointer is twisting and pulling the back weaver forward and over. You'll quickly get proficient at it!

15. As you finish the north-end spokes, move right around to the east ends and continue twining.

16. Make sure to twine in the spokes so none of them are crossing over each other in the center. Push the spokes so they are evenly spaced between the twines. It takes a little practice to get this looking uniform. Don't worry how your first attempts look. Just keep practicing.

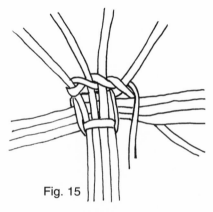

Fig. 15

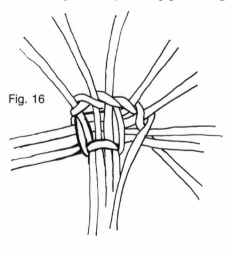

Fig. 16

17. Go all the way around. When you get back to the north ends, just keep going.

Fig. 17

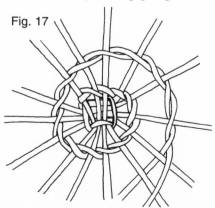

18. If you want to make a flat woven plate or tray, keep the start and spokes flat and just continue weaving. However, a basket requires a little push and shove against your leg to make it curve as you go around. Place the start (the side that was facing you), which will be the outside bottom of the basket, on your leg. As you twine, push the forming willows against your leg with pressure so the spokes bend upward and the twining tightens and holds the spokes in place. You will be working around the outside of the basket.

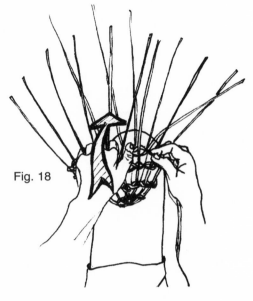

Fig. 18

Splicing. Now, it would be nice if you had the world's longest willows for weavers and could just twine around and around until your basket was finished. Unfortunately willows don't grow this long, and splicing is the inevitable and constant task of the basket weaver. You will certainly have to splice, even before you get to step 17, so here is the way to do it:

19. Always make sure the weaver you need to splice has its end behind the spoke. This is important so you can lock the splice into the weaving against the spoke.

20. Stick the fat end of the new willow shoot that is your splice downward along the right side of the spoke. The fat end of the new weaver will be angling down and slightly to the left. It will be in front of the short end of the old weaver and in back of the other weaver that doesn't need a splice yet.

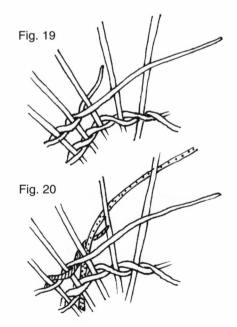

Fig. 19

Fig. 20

21. Pull the short end of the old weaver below the new weaver and then sharply up and in front so it wraps around it like a curled tendril. Let the short end of the old weaver, which is going upward, rest against the spoke.

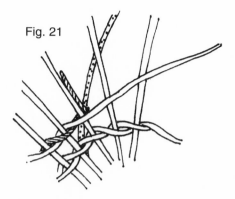

Fig. 21

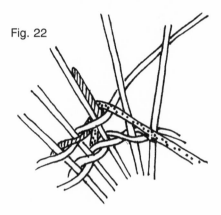

Fig. 22

22. Pull the new weaver forward and toward you so it comes over the other unspliced weaver.

23. This other unspliced weaver goes behind the next spoke, resting under the new splice. If this looks familiar, it is because it is the same twine you have been doing all along. Continue twining as before. Don't worry about the fat ends of your splices sticking into the basket wall. You can make it pretty by trimming the stubs when finished.

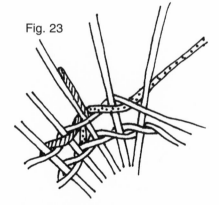

Fig. 23

Adding spokes. As your twining moves out along the initial 14 spokes, you need to add more spokes. Those first spokes splay out like the sun's rays after that first circle of twining is completed. If you continue twining without adding spokes, the spaces between the spokes will get larger and larger. If you like this effect and will only place large items in the basket, then you don't need to add spokes. However, if you want smaller and more consistent openings, then add spokes this way:

24. Cut 14 more shoots for spokes. Lay them along the right side of the original 14 spokes. Do this one at a time and shove each new spoke down into the lower twining so it is held in place next to the original spoke.

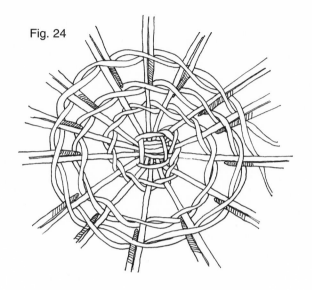

Fig. 24

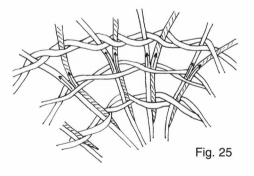

Fig. 25

25. For one more row, twine the weavers around the spokes without separating them. This weaves the spokes in more firmly. When you twine the weavers on the next row, split the spokes and twine each spoke individually. Now you have a row of 28 individually twined spokes. You can add another set of spokes if you want and continue to enlarge the basket, or you can reduce the number of spokes to bring the basket walls inward by twining every two spokes together as you go around one full row.

So, you've twined and spliced and added spokes and spliced and reduced and spliced or whatever you have wanted to do and spliced, spliced, spliced.

26. You are ready to finish the top edge of the basket. Your top edge looks like this:

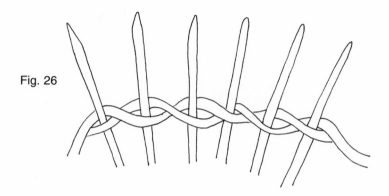

Fig. 26

27. Take any spoke and bend it sharply to the right, weaving it behind the spoke to the right of itself, in front of the second spoke to the right, and behind the third spoke to the right. Bend the spoke edge downward so it can be shoved down the twining on the right side of that third spoke. You may need to sharpen the end of the spoke and coax it downward.

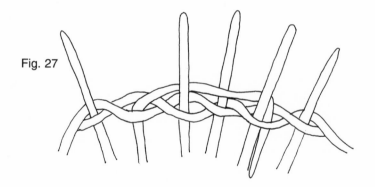

Fig. 27

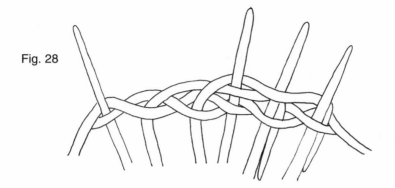

Fig. 28

28. When the first spoke is down, take the next spoke to the right side and weave it behind, in front, behind, and down.

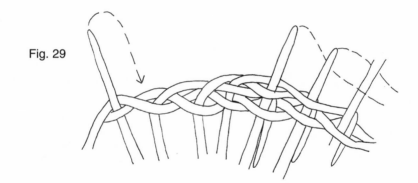

Fig. 29

29. Then weave the third spoke behind, in front, behind, down. Continue this all the way to the last spoke. Bend the last spoke down the hole where you first started to finish the top edge.

You are a basket weaver with a beautiful new basket!

Remember, guild meeting Thursday night!

CHAPTER 11

POTTERY

WE FIRST STARTED EXPERIMENTING WITH POTTERY while on southern desert courses. We saw pot shards and banks of clay all around us and decided to try our hand at clay cooking pots. Using number 10 food cans, or billy cans, didn't seem to fit with our hunter-gatherer curriculum of friction fires, coal beds, wild edibles, stone knives, and bark shelters. We had never taken a course in ceramics, but some questions to Chuck the geologist and Michael the clay sculptor, as well as a lot of trial and error, got us going.

Through experimentation we found that each clay has its own personality. Some are pure, and some need to be cleaned of rocks and organic matter. Most need to have some kind of *temper* added, such as sand, to keep the clay from cracking—cracking while drying, cracking while firing, and cracking while cooking! The more temper you add, the more resistant the pottery is to cracking; however, the temper makes the clay harder to work. Besides sand, other materials that can be used for temper are volcanic ash, burned shells (sea, mussel, or egg), and previously fired, crushed pottery pieces. The longer the clay has been wet, the easier it is to work. Some clays can only be successfully fired at low temperatures and some only at high temperatures requiring a kiln to contain the heat. Some won't fire at all.

We do not glaze our primitive pottery. Glaze is like molten glass during the firing, and ashes and charcoal stick to it, making a rough surface that is hard to keep clean and sanitary. Instead, the inside surface is finished as smooth as possible and polished before firing. Then it is easy to clean.

First you need to find a source of clay. Look in road cuts, streambeds, canyon walls, etc. Ask a geologist where to find clay in your region. If the clay needs to be cleaned, push it wet through a screen to remove twigs and stones. In our region, there are some very pure deposits that require no cleaning. We just grind the clay on the driveway with a cinder block, pour it through a screen, mix in some sand, and add water until the clay is the consistency of modeling clay. The ratio we use with our favorite deposit is two parts sand to five parts clay. This amount will vary and experimentation is required. At first we didn't use temper and had problems with larger pots cracking. Then we added some sand to the clay, and this worked well until the weather got hot and windy. Then the pots began to crack while drying. Finally we doubled the amount of sand, and even though initial workability suffered, after sitting in a sealed bucket for a week, the clay had regained enough flexibility that we could pinch it and coil it to make functional containers.

If you can't *find* clay, look up Ceramics in the phone book and buy some. It's pretty cheap. You'll want low-fire clay. We have had good luck with low-fire raku clay. We did have to add sand to one batch we bought, as it just wouldn't fire without cracking. You can usually buy it wet or dry. We recommend buying it wet since it will have had a chance to age and will be easier to shape.

Pinch Pots

Now you're ready to make something. Start small. Take a baseball-size piece and roll it around in your hands until it is smooth and round. Wet your thumb with water and stick it down in the middle of the ball. Now start pinching the sides out thinner. Go around and around, smoothing and thinning. You'll feel like you're back in kindergarten. Check the thickness of the bottom. If you leave it too thick, it might blow off in firing due to uneven heating. Enlarge the pot slowly, giving the clay a chance to stretch. If cracks form, wet them and smooth them back together.

After you've pinched a pot shape, refine its walls to an *even* thinness of between 1/4 and 1/2 inch (minimum and maximum). Wet your two first fingers and place them inside the pot. Use a wiping motion to thin the walls. Support the pot in the palm of your other hand as you do this.

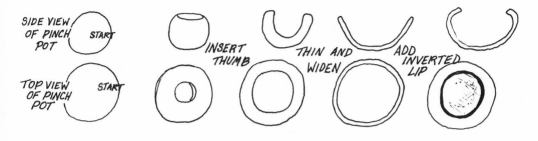

When the walls are consistent, turn in and work the top to finish the edge. You can add a coil to this edge to make a lip that will keep some ashes from blowing into the pot if you use it to cook over a fire. Wet the areas to be joined with a little water, and press the coil in firmly. Blend the coil into the top edge to eliminate cracks forming along this edge. Then wet your finger and smooth out the inside as best as you can to make it easier to keep clean later on.

Set the pot in a safe spot out of the sun and wind and let it dry. When the top lip is dry enough to support the weight of the pot, invert the pot so it is upside down to let the bottom dry. Flip-flop the pot a few times each day so it can dry evenly. The best way to prevent pots from cracking while drying is to dry them slowly. Pottery shrinks in size while drying, and uneven drying puts stress on the clay.

COIL POTS

You can make larger pots by building up coils of clay. Start with a small, dish-shaped base onto which you will add coils. Keep the top lip of the base a little fat (1/2 to 3/4 inch) to give a solid base for adding coils.

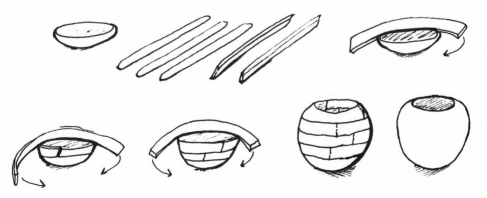

Roll out coils to a uniform thickness; then flatten them slightly and begin by joining them to the base, eventually spiraling up and up on top of each other. Coils applied at an inward angle will move the pot walls in, while coils applied at an outward angle will flare the walls out. After you put on a few coils, thin the walls somewhat, remembering to keep the lip a bit thick if you will be adding more coils.

Pots aren't the only things you can make out of clay. Kids love to make finger puppets. Beads are easy to make and always fire successfully. Check out Chapter 11 on music for clay flute ideas. Let your imagination go, but remember to avoid flat surfaces, as they are not as strong as rounded surfaces. Here are some tried and tested shapes that hold up well.

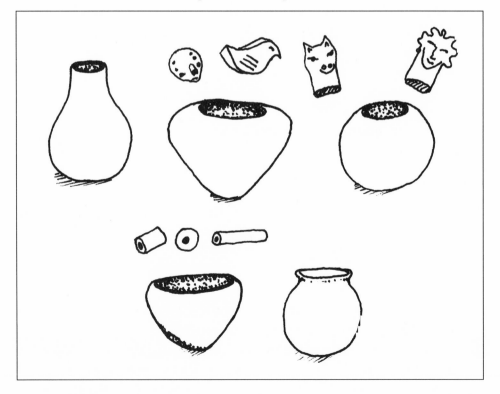

SLAB POTS

Large pots can also be built quickly using slabs of clay. It helps if you have an existing pot to use as a mold. Set the pot upside down and cover the outside with wet leaves or plastic.

Flatten a piece of clay; then cut it into a somewhat rectangular strip of a manageable size and flatten it. Press this slab onto the pot you are using for a mold. Start with the bottom and move out to the walls. Make another slab and join it to the first. Keep going until you have covered your bowl down to the point where it starts to turn inward. Stop here or you won't be able to get the clay off the mold.

The lip on the bottom still needs a final coil or two, so keep this unfinished edge damp while letting the base dry a bit on the mold. The base needs to be dry enough to support the weight of the pot, but if you leave the newly formed pot on the mold too long, it will shrink and crack.

So monitor this carefully, and when the base can support the weight, turn the pot onto its base. Remove the pot you used for a mold, remove the leaves or plastic from the inside of the new pot, and finish the top edge with a final coil or a series of coils to create a neck or other shape. Smooth the inside well and let the pot dry. The lip usually dries more quickly than the rest, so keep it covered with wet leaves. This will prevent cracking.

FINISHES

One way to smooth the inside of the pot (and this is important so as to make cleaning easy) is to **sand and burnish** it. (The outside can also be burnished, but with cooking vessels this isn't necessary.) When the pot is dry, sand the inside smooth using sandpaper or sand and a piece of buckskin. Pieces of sand in the temper will fall out. Don't worry about this.

When the pot has been sanded, paint the inside with a *slip* of clay. Stir a handful of clay with 1 quart water until it has liquified. Let the clay liquid settle to the bottom. Pour off the clear water on top and use the next layer as a slip. If you use different colors of clay you can make designs. (See Chapter 4 on color.) Paint this slip a little at a time on the sanded surface. As it dries, polish the surface with a very smooth rock or something similar. The pits where the temper fell out will eventually fill in with clay slip, and with enough polishing the surface will shine.

With some clays, however, adding slip won't work. It may flake off, or worse, the pot may crack. We don't have a hard and fast rule here; you'll have to experiment.

Using different-colored clay slips is not the only way to make designs. **Bee plant syrup** (described in Chapter 4 on color) can be made by a boiling process. Paint this dark syrup onto the pots when they are dry. The colors that will result after firing range from white, to black, to iridescent purple, depending on how much heat and oxygen get to your pot during firing.

Texturing is another design method. While drying, the outside of the pot can be textured by pressing in corn cobs, cord, your fingernails, etc. A textured surface makes it easier to grab the pot as well as increases surface area, which makes cooking faster. Remember, only add texture to the *outside* of the pot. You want the inside as smooth as possible.

REPAIRING CRACKS

If the pot cracks while drying, you can still save it. Lue Blankenship showed us this way of repairing cracks:

Carve the crack completely out of the pot with a knife. There will be a triangular hole in the pot wall. Mix vinegar with powdered clay till it is workable. Don't use water. Also dampen the crack with vinegar. Then fill the crack with this clay paste, using the knife. Compress the paste carefully and smooth it over with your finger. When the patch dries, smaller cracks may form. Cut these out and fill as before. It seems like a hassle, but it may keep you from punting your cracked pots or using them for batting practice. Once the clay is dry, sand the area lightly. Or you can wet it slightly and burnish as before.

FIRING

When the pot is finished and *totally* dry, it is ready for a firing. Do this on a calm day. Wind will heat or cool the pots too quickly, and the uneven temperature fluctuations will cause breakage. You can fire your pottery in a fireplace, a barbecue, or a campfire. Remember to check with the local fire department to see what's allowed. You'll need half a pickup full of old lumber for a campfire firing if using boards (check construction sites—they love you to cart off their scraps that would otherwise go to the landfill), or at least four large logs a foot in diameter and three feet long, plus some smaller wood to get it going. If you can talk a local farmer out of a few bushels of dried cow patties, you'll be all set. If you have no other choice, twenty pounds of charcoal will work.

Let's start with the barbecue. This one is simple. Put a layer of charcoal on the bottom; then put the pots in the middle. Put the rest of the charcoal on top and around. Mound the briquettes on the top, add a LITTLE lighter fluid on top, and light. Let it heat up slowly. Don't be tempted to squirt more lighter fluid as if you were going to cook something. You only want a couple of briquettes to get going on the top and for these to *slowly* catch the others on fire. When the briquettes really get going, put the lid on with vents fully open top and bottom. Let it burn itself out. The next day, when it is all cool, take out your pots. They should be hard enough that 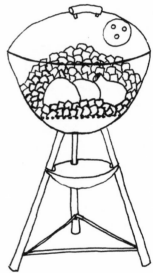 you can't easily scratch them with your fingernail. If not, you didn't get the heat high enough and you'll have to try firing them again. It may be that this particular clay only fires at higher temperatures than you can achieve without a kiln, napalm, or nuclear fusion, in which case you're out of luck for a home firing. In any case, the great amount of charcoal you have burned at once will have its effect elsewhere. Your poor barbecue will get very hot with this firing and the inside lining and outside paint will start to peel off. From then on the barbecue will start to rust. That's the bad news. The good news is that you'll never have to worry about anyone stealing the ugly thing!

If you have an old metal bucket that is large enough, you can put your

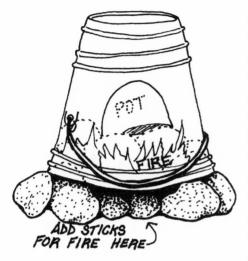

ADD STICKS
FOR FIRE HERE

pots up on some rocks and then put the bucket over these rock-supported pots as a lid. Leave room at the bottom to add fuel. Start a fire and add a few coals under the bucket. Gradually build up the fire under the bucket by adding sticks and coals. You want the fire to rage for a couple of hours. Then let it all cool down. This method uses little wood and may be the most inconspicuous way to fire outside if you don't have a barbecue. A word of caution: most metal buckets have a galvanized coating. This coating is toxic to breathe! Do this outside and stay downwind, or make another choice.

The next method uses a fireplace. Put the pots up on the grate and start a tiny fire on each side of the pots. Keep this fire going for an hour, and don't let the flames touch the pots. Then gradually move the fire closer and build it up so it is really going. However, don't let the flames leap up the chimney. Chimney fires burn down houses. Surround and cover the pots and burn fuel until the pots are glowing red for awhile. Then they are fired. Don't disturb the pots, coals, or ashes. Let them cool naturally.

The campfire method was shown to us by Evard Gibby. Put the pots up on a few rocks. Surround the pots with four big logs. Fill the resultant square with slow-burning combustible material such as dried cow dung, bark, charcoal, or whatever—something that will burn hot when it gets going, not something that will just smolder like leaves. Mound this up a foot or so above the pottery and start a small fire on top. The pots will heat up as the fire burns down. Eventually the big logs will catch and the fire will become intense. You can add wood carefully (avoid crushing the pots) until they glow red. Let the fire and pots cool naturally to avoid cracking.

This method has always worked well for us, except one time in Oregon when a thunderstorm whipped up just as the fire was lit. The wind preceding the rain was intense and the cow manure got hot so quickly that *all* the pots broke! We were camping at Glass Buttes, which is a mountain of obsidian. When we dug out the broken debris, we discovered some silver-sheen obsidian that had been in the bottom of the pit. The silver sheen had literally boiled out of the obsidian due to the intense heat!

The final method is one we call the ring of fire. It has provided us with the most success but is also the most wood-consumptive process. Put the pottery up on rocks a few inches above the ground. Build a fire around the pottery and hold the fire there for two hours. Don't let the flames touch the pottery. If you have anything that you can use to shield the pottery, this will help. We have used slabs of rock and broken pieces of fired pottery; some people use scrap pieces of metal, etc. After two hours, you can (but don't have to) add some insulating material that will burn, such as cow patties, all around the pottery. This will slow the heating-up process of the pots during the firing. Without insulating material, be sure to do the next step more slowly. Push the fire in toward the center where the pots are. Add more wood and let it burn. (Dry wood makes less smoke.) When the pots are glowing

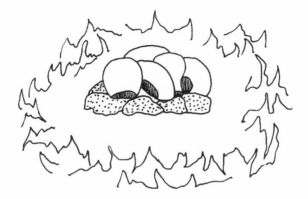

red, they are fired and can be allowed to cool naturally. Glowing red pots are difficult to see in the daylight, so if the fire has been raging for a couple of hours, you can feel confident that you have gotten it hot enough—this is, of course, if you are using a low-fire clay.

Sometimes we do a **reduction firing to get shiny, jet-black pottery.** (This is a firing that reduces oxygen to the pottery and turns the pots black.) The result is very beautiful. All this is cosmetic, and we don't do this for cooking pots. Cooking pots can change color when you use them. To get this look, first burnish the outside of the pot when it is leather-hard with a very smooth stone, or dampen the dried pottery a little at a time and burnish this

damp spot. It will shine as you do this. Then, when firing, pile on dry, powdered cow manure or dry, rotten wood once the pots are glowing red. Immediately suffocate the fire with dirt. Let it cool naturally. It may even take a full day to cool this way, but the results are quite beautiful. The pots will look like they have a black glaze.

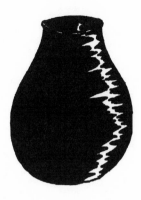

Now, remember, pottery without a glaze will sweat—allow water to leak through its pores. This keeps stored water cooler. But for cooking, you need a sealed container. Do this the first time you use the pot by cooking something starchy such as oatmeal. After that, the pot will be watertight.

Now you have several methods to fire your pottery, even in the city, which is a large part of what this book is about. You will be able to cook great meals in your pots. (See Chapter 7 on cooking). And there is nothing like sipping tea from a rounded cup that fits your hands, the hands that fashioned it from the earth, letting the warmth of the tea move through the clay and into your fingers as you watch the snow come down.

So there you have it, making pots from dirt. Now go out and dig up some clay!

CHAPTER 11

FOOD AND COOKING

THERE ARE REALLY ONLY THREE ESSENTIALS IN LIFE. We list them in order of importance like this: love, water, food. The best food usually incorporates the first. Even the simplest foods, prepared lovingly, seem somehow more nourishing and satisfying. And when you gather and prepare foods yourself and cook them in containers you have made, the nourishment goes beyond the bodily type.

Food is all around us in nature at all times of the year. We have forgotten how to recognize this abundant food source as we have become more and more accustomed to food coming from a cardboard box or plastic bag, or from behind the deli counter. Once you begin to recognize food in its natural and seasonal states, you'll be amazed at the bounty, even in the most urban areas. You'll see food in backyards, in front of the new office park, on the corner by the bank, growing in a window flower box and along the road going to the next town.

We have planned four seasonal meals that incorporate wild foods and Stone Age cooking methods into a modern diet with modern cooking methods. We are sharing recipes that we use all the time. You'll probably recognize most of the ingredients, but if you come across something new, get a good field guide and start practicing. Recipes for jellies and directions for drying, jerking, and smoking will come at the end of the chapter.

A word about meat. Vegetarians will find many delightful and delicious recipes in the next few pages. Some of the recipes include fish, turkey, and wild game. If you don't eat meat, just exclude these recipes from the menu and the meals will still stand on their own. The wild grains are high in protein, as is acorn meal. Meat eaters will be delighted at the flavor and leanness of the wild game. We hunt with respect, taking responsibility for the choice to eat meat. There are no chemicals, colorings, or steroids in our meat. It's hard not to enjoy something that is obtained, prepared, and served in reverence.

You don't have to be a hunter to enjoy wild game. Hook up with someone in your area who does hunt, and agree to help with hunting-camp chores or meals, haul camp gear, carry out meat, or help tan the buckskin after the hunt in exchange for some of the meat.

We are the kind of cooks who go to the kitchen and throw it all together. We rarely follow a recipe, and when we do we don't measure very carefully. The spirit of this cooking style is reflected in these recipes. Have fun and allow the "half jar of this," the "dash of that," the "spoonful of such and such" to free your creative cooking talents.

SPRING FOODS

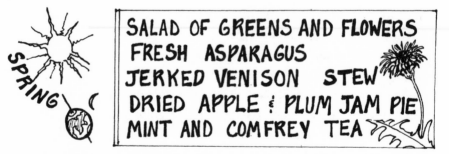

SALAD OF GREENS AND FLOWERS
FRESH ASPARAGUS
JERKED VENISON STEW
DRIED APPLE & PLUM JAM PIE
MINT AND COMFREY TEA

Let's start with the newness of spring! Spring is the time for finishing up the preserved foods in the cupboard and for gathering the tender shoots and new growth of nature.

Our spring meal begins with the **salad.**

Young dandelion leaves from plants that have not flowered

Violet flowers

Pennycress mustard leaves and flowers

New curly dock leaves
Small mint leaves

Gather more dandelion leaves and violets than other plants, and add any other produce you want. Grapes and cucumbers go very well. The flavors are so pleasing and distinct that no dressing is needed. Toss everything together and serve.

Asparagus heralds spring with its light green shoots. It grows everywhere, usually along fence lines and roadsides. Gather the shoots only. Steam and serve. You'll find the flavor of wild asparagus full and satisfying. There is no need for salt or butter.

Jerked-venison stew needs to cook slowly throughout the day. Even so, you'll want to soak the meat in water, a dribble of red wine vinegar, and a sprinkle of crushed black pepper overnight. In the morning, put the meat and juice in a pot and cover it with more water. Cook until the meat is soft. Add fresh, whole wild onions and a few mustard leaves. Celery, carrots, turnips, spring beauty bulbs, potatoes, or squash are all good additions. Cook until all your ingredients are soft. Add a dash of mace, a sprinkle of allspice, a spoonful of blackstrap molasses, and 3 or 4 fresh tomatoes chopped in chunks. Cook another half hour. Serve.

Dried apples and plum jam pie is a great way to use the fruits that you preserved the previous fall. Soak the apples overnight in water. When they are well hydrated, drain the water and add half a jar of plum jam. Cook this apple-plum mixture over low heat and sprinkle in some raisins if you want. Add a tiny dash of crushed clove. Cook to let this thicken, adding a small spoon of cornstarch if it's too runny. Pour the filling into a pie shell and bake for 10 minutes at 450 degrees, then 40 more minutes at 350 degrees.

If you bake over a fire, set the pie pan on a bed of hot, level coals and cover it with a well-fitting lid. Shovel a pile of coals on top of the lid. If the pan is close to the flames, rotate it so one side of the crust doesn't burn. The pie is done when the filling is bubbling and the crust is golden.

Mint and comfrey tea is a cheerful accompaniment to the pie. You will find baby leaves from both these plants in spring. Rip the leaves into pieces. (Use more mint than comfrey.) Pour boiled water over them and let sit. Strain and serve. A perfect compliment to apple-plum pie!

Summer Foods

SALAD OF GREENS AND FLOWERS
CORN ON THE COB
COAL-BAKED FISH
PUFF BREAD
FRESH BERRY COBBLER
ICED SORREL TEA

The abundance of summer is cause for celebration. Here's a summer meal that does it up right!

Salad:
Nasturtium blossoms
Sweet William blossoms
Pigweed leaves
Lamb's-quarter leaves
Bluebell flowers and leaves
Mustard greens

Mix everything together and set a bright nasturtium blossom on the center top. Once again, the delightful flavors make dressing unnecessary.

Corn on the cob can be roasted on the coals inside its own husk. No need for tin foil. We soak the corn and husk in water for an hour or so, then drain well with the silks down. Lay the cobs on the coal bed and cook about 15 minutes. This cooking method gives corn a slight nutty flavor. You won't need salt or butter.

Fish cooked over the coals should be gutted but not scaled. This will protect the meat. Leave the head on until it is cooked, as this keeps the top end of the meat cleaner. (Larger fish have two nice chunks of cheek meat in the head. Try it.) Make slits down the outside of the fish every inch or so that run to the backbone. Sprinkle any variety of spices that you like into the slits. Place the fish directly on the coals, and cook until the meat is no longer translucent. Turn gently and cook the opposite side. The fish will arch as it cooks. Try to keep it in contact with the coals so it cooks evenly. When it's done, remove the head and tail, peel off the skin, and eat.

Make up a quick dough for **puff bread** while the fish and corn are cooking. Mix a bowl of flour together with a small spoon of salt and two large spoons of baking powder. Set half of this dry mix aside to make dessert. Add a little water to the remaining half until the dough is easy to pat out but not at all tacky. Pat the dough into little tortilla shapes. Place these directly on the coals. They will puff up and crisp, turning  golden. You can also cook these on a large flat rock slab propped over the fire on support rocks. They are great with honey, and summer is honey season!

A glass of **iced sorrel or staghorn sumac tea,** sweetened with a dab of honey or straight up for those who like it tart, is a great summer drink. Pick the flowering heads of the sorrel or berries of the sumac and put them in a jar. Fill the jar with water and set in the sun. After a few hours, pour the strained tea over ice and garnish with a sprig of mint.

Berry cobbler is a terrific summer dessert. All kinds of berries are ripe. You can mix and match or stick to one kind. We love raspberry and currant or huckleberry and strawberry mixed together.

Mash half of the berries and get a good juice going. Add some water and a little honey. Put the rest of the berries into the juice. You want this berry juice to fill at least the bottom third of the pot. To the flour mix you reserved from making the puff bread, add water until the consistency is like biscuit dough. (Since these are drop biscuits, the consistency can be a little gooey.) Drop the dough by spoonfuls onto the berry juice. In the oven, bake at 400 degrees for about 25 minutes, until the cobbler top is golden. On the fire, use a pan with a lid, a dutch oven, or a pottery bowl and lid, and follow the same procedure for baking on the coals as described in making the spring pie. (When using pottery, let the coals build up slowly around the dish to avoid thermal shock and cracking. Scoop a few coals at a time from the fire and gradually increase the coals under, on, and around the pot.) It is done when a knife or other object inserted in the middle of the cobbler crust comes out clean.

FALL FOODS

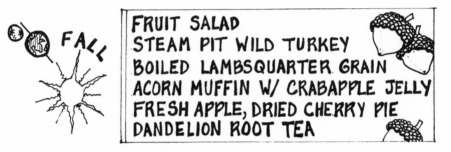

```
FRUIT SALAD
STEAM PIT WILD TURKEY
BOILED LAMBSQUARTER GRAIN
ACORN MUFFIN W/ CRABAPPLE JELLY
FRESH APPLE, DRIED CHERRY PIE
DANDELION ROOT TEA
```

Fall is the season for harvesting abundantly and preserving summer foods for use in winter and early spring. So many things are ripe and ready in fall that it is easy to come up with a delectable feast.

A sliced fruit salad is a great start. Where we live, wild peaches are ready at the end of September or early October, as well as apples, grapes, and pears. We also rove the neighborhoods and ask folks if we can pick from their vines and trees. We always leave some fresh-picked fruits on the doorstep and be sure to return a few weeks later with a jar of jelly or a pie. Slice up whatever fruit you have collected and mix it all together. Serve.

Acorn muffins are a gift from the gods. Our favorite acorns come from white, live, and burr oaks. They are only slightly bitter and require less leaching than acorns from red, gambels, and black oaks. These latter varieties have more tannic acid and need more processing. Nevertheless this is a simple process and the end results are terrific.

Oaks grow, in one form or another, just about everywhere. Gather, decap, and shell the acorns. Grind them into a flour meal consistency. We use large rounded stream rocks on our front porch, which is a stone slab, for grind-

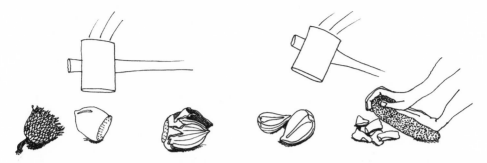

ing. Put the meal in a large pot and fill the pot with water. Let it settle. Depending on the bitterness of the acorns, pour off the water and repeat this process as often as necessary until the meal loses its bitter taste. If this is taking a long time, set it in the refrigerator or in some other cool place so the meal doesn't spoil. When the meal is leached and well drained, it is ready to use.

Mix:

3/4 cup of acorn meal

1 cup white, wheat, lamb's-quarter, or amaranth flour (or any combination mixed together)

1/3 cup turbinado sugar or 1/2 cup honey

1/2 teaspoon salt

1 tablespoon of baking powder

Add in:

1 egg (optional)

1 cup milk or water

2 tablespoons melted butter or rendered elk fat

Blend well. Fill greased muffin tins and bake at 425 degrees for 15 to 20 minutes. Serve the acorn muffins with crabapple jelly. (See end of chapter for jelly-making directions.)

Wild turkey cooked in a steam pit is an autumn treat. For a 10-pound turkey, prepare the pit and the turkey 9 hours before your planned meal. First, dig a hole in the ground about 2 feet deep and 2 feet across. Start a fire in the hole and get it burning with lots of wood that will make good coals. Throw in 10-15 rocks about the size of grapefruit. (Don't use river rocks because they explode!) Let the fire burn seriously for a few hours. If the ground is very wet, add an hour or so to the burning time.

While the fire is burning in the pit, gather enough wet grass or other vegetation to provide two 3-inch layers in the pit. Also pluck and clean the turkey. Save the appropriate innards to make gravy. Plucking is a snap if you dip the bird in a pot of boiling water first. Pluck quickly. If the bird cools off, redip. Rub the bird with your favorite spices and wrap it in an all-natural fiber bag that won't melt or discolor. Untreated burlap works well. (For a delicious variation, try stuffing the bird with bread cubes and sweet sicily.)

Lay 3 inches of wet grass on top of the coals and rocks. Lay the bagged turkey on top of this grass. If you want to throw in potatoes, carrots, beets, rutabagas, or whatever, place them in a bag as well and set them out in a layer over the grass. Cover the food with another 3-inch layer of grass, then cover the grass with the dirt you dug out of the pit. Mound all of the dirt up on the top of the pit and generously around the top edges to prevent heat loss. Let cook about 7 hours for a 10-pound turkey. Don't worry about overcooking; the longer the turkey cooks by this method, the more tender it will be.

Dig up the bag. The meat will be succulent and falling off the bone. You can use your steam-pit cooking site over and over again.

A steaming bowl of grains goes well with the turkey. Lamb's-quarter seed, amaranth, or golden head grass seed can be easily collected by shaking the ripe seed heads into a paper bag or by pulling your hand along the stalk and collecting the seed in your hand.

Pick up seed and chaff and hold a container one foot below. As you slowly drop seeds and chaff, a gentle breeze will blow the lighter chaff away as the heavier seeds fall into the container. If there is no breeze, simply walk slowly while dropping the seeds over the container. This will create a breeze to separate the two.

Boil the grains in water and drain. Make turkey gravy from the innards you saved and pour it over the grains.

A fresh-apple-and-dried-cherry pie, sweetened with apple juice concentrate, makes a lovely finale to your autumn meal.

Slice and core the apples. (We don't peel ours.) Add dried cherry halves that you would have harvested in July. Or, you can pick rose hips, split them open, and clean out the seeds and fuzz. Mix in 1/2 can of apple juice concentrate and a small spoonful of cornstarch. Cook this over the heat until it thickens slightly, then pour it into a pie crust and bake at 450 degrees for 10 minutes and then at 350 degrees for 40 minutes more, or until the juices are boiling. You can also bake this pie on the fire, of course.

Dandelion root tea is a flavorful accompaniment to the meal. You will have dug the dandelion roots in the spring and early summer, washed and split them in half lengthwise, roasted them in a slow oven until they were light brown, let them cool and dry thoroughly, and now be pulling those roots out for use. To make tea, mash them lightly and pour boiled water over them. Strain and serve. The tea is dark, with a robust flavor.

WINTER FOODS

HOT-ROCK PUMPKIN SOUP
SMOKED ELK SAUSAGE
CATTAIL POLLEN BISCUIT
ACORN FRITTER ROLLED IN CINNAMON
PINE NEEDLE TEA

Winter meals are flavorful and earthy. Here's a satisfying menu for short days and long nights.

A hearty pumpkin soup is a great way to start off a winter feed. It's also a lot of fun to use the pumpkin as your cooking container. We do this by hot-rock cooking in the pumpkin! As the soup cooks, the pumpkin flesh is cooking too. When the soup is done, you can fill your bowl and then scoop out a generous spoon of pumpkin flesh, cooked to perfection in the soup juices. Mmm . . .

Build a fire and let a good coal bed build up. (You can do this in your fireplace, too.) Put 14 small round rocks about 2 inches across into the fire. Choose rocks that are not gritty but smooth, and have not come from a river or streambed. While the rocks are heating, cut open the top of a large pumpkin, just like you would to start a jack-o-lantern, and clean out the insides. Save the seeds for roasting or steaming.

Choose your ingredients for the soup. Our last pumpkin soup had nettle leaves, beet leaves, onion, fresh garlic, potatoes, dried tomato, carrots, and chunks of elk meat. We spiced with molasses, white wine, cracked pepper, and basil.

Place the ingredients in the pumpkin, then pour in water until the pumpkin is 2/3 full. Take the hot rocks out of the fire one at a time, blow off the ashes, and drop them into the soup. After about 7 or 8 rocks, the water will be boiling furiously and the pumpkin will begin vibrating! The form-fitting pumpkin lid helps contain the heat. Let the soup cook until the boiling fades to a simmer and the simmering stops. Fish the rocks out of the soup and put them back into the fire. Add the remaining hot rocks to the soup. These should keep the soup boiling about 25 to 30 minutes. This is a very efficient way to cook!

Fish out the second batch of rocks and put the reheated batch in again. By the time the soup stops simmering on this round, it should be ready to serve. Top the served soup with a generous scraping of the cooked pumpkin flesh.

Cattail-pollen-and-deer-fat biscuits are flaky and flavorful. You will have collected the cattail pollen in the summer. To do this, hold a large paper bag over the cattail heads, bend the stalk gently downward, grip the bag closed around the base of the cattail head and shake vigorously. Repeat this until you have the amount of cattail pollen flour you want.

Mix 1 cup of cattail flour with 2 cups of any other flour you want and fill a small bowl. Add one heaping tablespoon of baking powder and a pinch of salt to the flour. Mix together well. Cut in two heaping tablespoons of rendered deer or elk fat until fine little pea shapes form. Slowly add a little milk or cold water and beat until a soft dough forms. It should not be sticky. Roll or pat the dough into a 3/4-inch layer, then cut out circles. Grease a cookie sheet and place the biscuit rounds on the sheet with their sides touching. Bake at 425 degrees until golden brown.

Smoked elk sausages make a perfect winter side dish. Follow this recipe:

3 pounds elk meat, coarse ground

In a small bowl mix:

1 3/4 teaspoons pepper

1 1/2 teaspoons salt

1/2 teaspoon dry mustard

1/2 teaspoon mace

3/4 teaspoon sugar

1/2 teaspoon crushed marjoram

1/2 teaspoon nutmeg

Sprinkle the mixed spices over the meat and mix them in with your hands. Grind the spiced meat again. Stuff into cleaned intestine or purchased hank. The sausage is ready to smoke.

Elk is very lean, so if you decide to cook the sausage without smoking, be sure to add a 1/2 cup water to the pan. For a final browning, either drain the water from the pan or roast gently over a fire. If you smoke the sausages, heat them for serving by dropping them into boiling water, or boil, cool, and serve them cold and sliced.

Pine needle tea is abundantly available and can be made fresh all winter, as well as any other time of year. Strip the needles from the branch and break them in two. Pour boiled water over the needles and let steep. By not boiling the needles in the water you preserve vitamins C and B. Adding a heaping spoon of hot cocoa mix makes a tasty variation.

Acorn fritters are a delicious dessert to finish your meal. Mix a cup of acorn meal with a cup of flour, a teaspoon of baking powder, and a pinch of salt. Beat one egg and add 1/3 cup of milk. Mix everything together. Drop the batter by spoonfuls into deep fat and fry. Drain on a paper bag. Roll in cinnamon and powdered sugar.

FOOD PRESERVATION TECHNIQUES

To dry apples: Core the apples. Slice them sideways so the slices are round rings with the core hole in the center. String the slices on a cord and hang in a dry, sunny place. When they are completely dry, store them in cloth or paper bags or in glass canning jars with loose-fitting lids.

To dry cherries: Split the cherries in half and remove the pits. Lay them skin side down on woven trays or racks that allow air to get to the bottom of the cherries. Set in a sunny window. When the cherries are completely dry, store the same as apples.

To make plum jam: Mash the plums and put them into the pot with skins and pits. Pectin is concentrated in the skins and pits. The combination of pectin and sugar is what allows the fruit to jell.

Simmer the plums until they are soft and then run them through a food strainer to remove the pits and skins. In a large pot, combine 5-1/2 cups of the plum mush with 5 cups of sugar. Bring to a full boil and let boil hard for 1 minute, stirring constantly. You'll get about 5 pints. Pour into hot, clean jars. Leave 1/4 inch of head space. Seal the jars with caps and rings you have simmered first. Tighten the rings and invert the jars for 15 minutes. Turn upright and let cool. Test your seals. Don't store anything that hasn't sealed.

You can make a small batch of jelly over the fire for immediate use. High-pectin fruits such as plums, crabapples, grapes, currants, gooseberries, and apples don't need pectin and require less sugar to jell. We have had good results using juice concentrate instead of sugar with high-pectin fruits. If your jam doesn't jell, use it for syrup or dessert topping. Cook the jam in small batches for consistent jelling success.

To make crabapple jelly: Cook whole crabapples, stems and all, until soft. Run through a food strainer to remove the skins, stems, and seeds. Mix four cups of crabapple juice and 4 cups of sugar. Boil hard. When you can dip a spoon sideways in the boiling mixture and the jelly falls off the spoon in a curtain instead of dripping from a point, the jelly is ready to be poured into clean, hot jars. You'll get about three pints. Follow the previous directions for sealing.

To jerk meat: Cut meat into strips thinner than 1/4 inch. It is easier to slice thin if the meat has been frozen and then slightly thawed. Lay on woven trays or steel-mesh screens, or make a wooden frame to support a piece of cheesecloth pulled taut. Cover the meat strips with one of these three choices as well. Your meat is safe from flying bugs and can dry quickly. When the strips are completely dry, store in a cloth or paper bag, a pottery or gourd bowl with a lid, or in a glass jar.

To render fat: Cut the collected fat into little bits. Put it in a pot for boiling and cover with water. (Do this outside so you don't coat your home in grease and attract bugs.) Boil the fat until it is liquid. You may need to add more water so the fat doesn't scorch. When the fat has liquefied, scoop out anything still floating and then let the fat cool. The cool fat will form a solid cake on the surface. Lift the cake and scrape off any impurities on the bottom surface. Keep rendered fat in a cool, dark place to prevent spoiling. It can be used for biscuits and pie crusts, as well as greasing and frying.

Rendered fat has lots of other uses besides cooking. Make a candle by filling a small pot with fat and inserting a cord wick. Cook the rendered fat without water. When it cools, it will be waxy. Use it to grease footwear. Even if you don't eat animals, you may find uses for animal products like these.

To smoke sausage: If you want to preserve your food with smoke, you must use a cool smoke, not hotter than 90 degrees, and smoke long enough for a thick rind to build up on the food. This takes time and care, but it is an excellent preservation method for meats, poultry, and fish. If you are smoking only for flavor, you can use a hotter smoke and less time. However, meat smoked this way will have been slightly cooked and will not keep; it requires refrigeration or freezing.

You can smoke over the fire, but it is more efficient to build a little smoke box. Use wood, buckskin, canvas, or scrap metal to make a small enclosed area where the smoke can concentrate. Make a small upper vent for circulation. Have steel or woven racks to set your sausage on inside the enclosed area. If you weave racks, soak them in water before smoking. Make a small place for the smoky fire under the racks, where you can easily reach in to add wood or wet hardwood chips without losing a lot of smoke. Having a small wood stove with the pipe funneled into the bottom of the smoke box works well, too. Have you ever tried smoked peaches? No time like the present!

Take a closer look at the recipes and cooking methods in this chapter. You'll notice that the cooking methods keep you active in food gathering and preparation. You'll also notice the recipes contain a large variety of foods that provide a huge range of vitamins and minerals, lack saturated fat, are high in fiber and low in cholesterol and salt. They have incredible appetite appeal. We didn't try to select the recipes and methods to provide these things. This is the nature of wild foods and old preparation methods. Your body has evolved for millions of years to eat and move in these ways, and as you begin reincorporating these techniques into your modern lifestyle, you'll see your body respond. Sumptuous meals aren't the only reward for "going paleo" in the kitchen! Bon appetit!

CHAPTER

SOAP

BEING ALL WASHED UP—CLEAN, NEAT, AND TIDY—are hardly ideas we associate with the primitive, barbarian, or caveman. However, there are several reasons why early people needed to be clean. Then, as now, cuts, wounds, and rashes all need to be cleansed of bacteria to prevent infections. Being as scent free as possible helps to avoid alerting game in hunting. Food, as well as eating and cooking gear, needs to be kept clean to keep healthy. We learned all these things at an early time or wouldn't have survived as a species.

Plants that can be used for cleansing could be a whole book in itself. We're going to keep it simple and list three plants that contain saponin, an effective sudsy cleanser. These are bouncing bet (also called soapwort), clematis, and yucca. These soaps will make a natural addition to your cleaning cupboard. However, before you use any plant, you need to test it to see if you are allergic to it. Once we tried some agave for soap and developed a rash. It itched like fire at first; in a couple of days it subsided. Now we use caution with anything we haven't tried before. When using any product on your skin for the first time, it is wise to test for allergic reactions by placing a drop on the inside of the wrist. If no reaction occurs by the next day, you should be able to use the plants for soap.

Following are a variety of plants that yield soap:

Bouncing Bet. Collect bouncing bet from late summer to fall, even after its flowers have disappeared. It is found nationwide, is a showy flower with five petals, and is often cultivated. The flowers can be white or pink. The whole plant can be used, but it is easier to find while in bloom. When we tried to use specimens collected before flowering, we didn't get any suds. Dried and dead plants do work, however.

This makes a good soap for hand washing and other household uses. Just one plant gets hands squeaky clean. *Don't use bouncing bet on face or hair because it really irritates the eyes.*

Clematis is a common climbing vine that dominates the tops of many trees. Its flowers are white or purple; in the fall they seed and turn into long, wispy fluff. Collect the leaves and

flowers off the vine. The amount of soapiness in individual plants varies greatly. Experiment to get the amount of suds you need.

The large, woody vines of clematis are also good for starting friction fires (see Chapter 1 on fire).

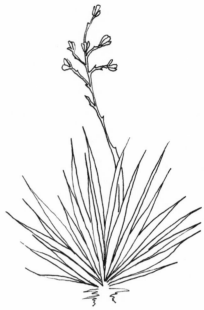

Yucca and its relatives, **agave, Spanish bayonet, sotol, Joshua tree,** etc., contain saponin. This is present throughout the plant, but we find the root easiest to process. This kills the plant, so use as much of the plant as you can and don't waste. The leaves can be used for cordage and the flower stalk for starting friction fires. The flowers are edible too, although some flowers will taste too soapy. This plant is found in dry areas and is easily recognizable by its spiky leaves. Yucca is the mildest soap we have used, and is good for hair, face, and bathing. One whole plant makes an extravagant green bubble bath. Just pound and soak the leaves of yucca in preparation for making cording fiber and then pour the fresh soaking water into the tub and run your bath!

HOW TO MAKE SOAP

To make soap suds from any of these plants, chop up, grate, or crush the part of the plant you want to use. This can be used right away or dried for later use. To use, just rub between your hands with a small amount of water to get suds. If you want to wash your hair, crush some of the plant, wet your hair, rub the plant into your hair to lather, let soak for a minute, and rinse. Repeat as necessary.

Remember to use the soaps away from streams and lakes, as saponin will break down the surface tension of water, destroying habitat for a whole world of tiny critters and plants that live in this tension layer.

So, now you know some easy-to-find soap plants to get you started. As you walk through town or take a hike, keep your eyes open for these plants. They are a quick and simple aid to getting all washed up. Happy sudsing!

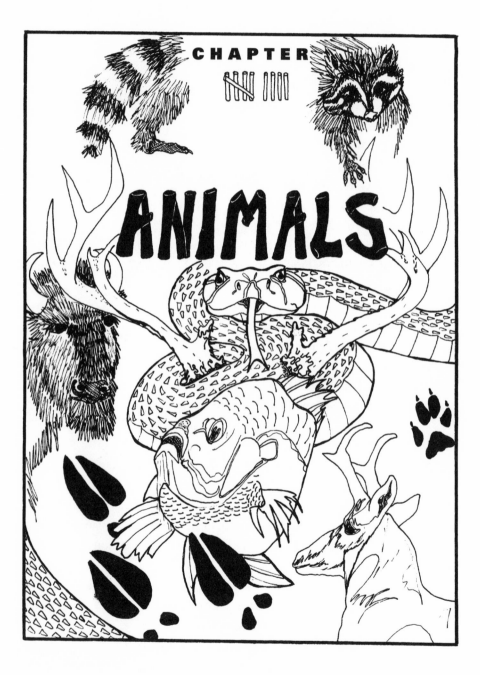

CHAPTER IIII

ANIMALS

IT HAS BEEN SAID THAT MAMMOTHS, BUFFALOES, AND OTHER ANIMALS in the past were, to our hunter-gatherer predecessors, as shopping malls are to us. Certainly the animals provided for many needs. And although this comparison helps to open our minds to the amazing resources that animals offered, it superimposes a modern consumer mentality upon our ancestors. This perspective fails to include the alligator rushing into muddy water, the cornered mouse baring its teeth in fierce self-defense, the mountain goat springing from crack to crevice on a cliff face, and the squirrel jumping breathtakingly from tree limb to tree limb.

Have you ever been stopped in your tracks by the cry of a hawk? Or come face to face with an eighty-pound grouper whose "thump, thump" means "back off"? Have you ever been stilled into observation by the order and persistence of a line of ants? Have you stood in awe before the beating of the hummingbird's wing?

When the vitality and determination of other beings are seen, respect and reverence are natural responses. Animals are not consumption units. They are fellow beings who all contribute—along with the trees, the plants, the wind, the water, the rocks, and the dirt—a piece of what makes this world livable. We are all part of the big picture.

It is from this perspective that we put forward these ideas on using what the animals offer us. For many of us, this close connection with animals makes it difficult to think of using the animal parts. Others may simply find it completely unappealing. But when so many animals die as a direct result of collision, sometimes literally, with modern lifestyles, it then seems to make sense to take the opportunity to use this final offering in a useful way.

There are many ways to obtain animal parts without being involved in hunting. If you don't hunt, you may find hunters who will gladly save sinew, bones, hides, or other useful items. Butchers who process wild game often have hides and other parts to sell. And there is always the animal killed on the highway that begs to be put to use.

Besides providing meat, the animal carcass has scores of other uses. We make hides into rawhide or buckskin and render the fat for shortening, fat lamps, and waterproofing. Sinew is great for lashing and thread. From bones we make hide scrapers, awls, needles, fish hooks, net shuttles, and buttons. Antlers become buttons too, as well as stoneworking tools and wedges for splitting wood. Hollowed hooves make great rattles. We stuff the cleaned intestines to make sausage, use the brains for tanning, and use gunnysacks stuffed with hair for target practice with our stone-tipped arrows. Hide scraps and scrapings make glue. Teeth and claws we use for decoration. Furbearers that we find on the road are made into hats, coats, and trim; and flattened snakeskins are glued to the backs of our sinew-strengthened bows for water-proofing as well as for camouflage.

Throughout the book you will find directions for making many things from animal parts. In this chapter we address the tanning of furs and buck-skin, and making rawhide.

SKINNING THE ANIMAL

Start small, say, with a raccoon. That way you can have success without getting in too deep. You will need a sharp knife, a smooth log, a drawknife (or in a pinch, a large butcher's knife), a pot, and a rope or cable.

Start by skinning the animal. Make cuts just through the skin along the inside of the legs, up the belly, and around the wrists. Hang the animal by a back leg and by pulling and cutting, undress it. Places that are tricky are the rump area (the skin sticks to the meat here) and tail. Cut along the under-side of the tail, and cut and peel the skin down. A wise 10th Mountain

Division soldier, Har, gave us this tip: Once the top of the tailbone is exposed, take a stick an inch in diameter and split one end down four inches. Put the tailbone in this split, grip the stick on both sides and pull. The skin will come off the bone. Now split the tail to the tip along the underside.

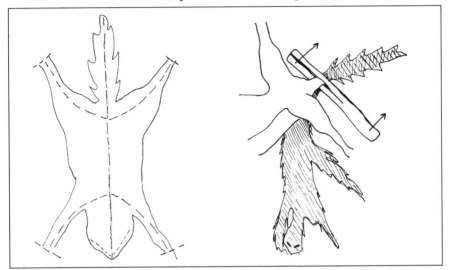

Skinning around the head can also be difficult. You will need to cut through ear cartilage, and take care not to enlarge the eyes. Skin out to the nose, and then you are ready to flesh the animal.

If there are fleas or ticks, you can put the fur in the freezer for a couple of days to kill them. This is also a good way to store fresh hides until you can take the time to process them. Otherwise, you will need to flesh them and hang them to dry. Unroll the edges to avoid rotting as they dry.

We do not tan hides with any artificial chemicals. All our tanning is brain tanning. You will need to remove the brains from the head and save them in the freezer for later use.

SCRAPING THE HIDE

Lean a smooth log up against a tree for fleshing the hide. (Instructions for making a fleshing beam are in Chapter 3 on tools.) Now place the hide on the beam, hair side down. Pinch the head of the hide between the beam and the tree to keep the hide from slipping down while you scrape.

Remove the meat and fat clinging to the flesh side of the hide with downward scraping of a drawknife or butcher knife. When you have worked all you can in one place, shift the skin, putting another portion behind the beam, and keep working until all the flesh and fat are removed. Liquid fat will actually squeeze out of tiny pockets in the hide, especially on coyotes, raccoons, skunks, and bears. It is good to get as much fat out of the hide as possible because too much fat left in the hide can cause it to break down in the future. It will be a little tricky on the tail and the head. Having a partner to hold the skin apart will help. When you have finished, the skin should be white.

Now get a bucket of warm, soapy water and give the skin a good washing. This will get out any dirt, blood, and much of the heavy scent. Rinse the skin, squeeze out the water, and then give it a shake. Sew up any holes now and hang the skin, fur side toward the sun, to dry a bit.

TANNING

Fur tanning without brains. For raccoons, we have the best luck tanning without adding brains. When the skin dries to a yellow color but is still wet enough to be stretched, work the skin by pulling the flesh side back and forth across a rope or eighth-inch cable. It will turn white again. This rope or cable should be stretched tightly, vertically between a limb and a tree trunk. You don't have to work the hide constantly. As it dries, feel where it is getting stiff and pull it there. Rotate your grip 90 degrees and pull in the same place. This stretches the fibers, pulling them across each other. The hide is actually glue (see Chapter 10 on glue) that is striving to glue the fibers of 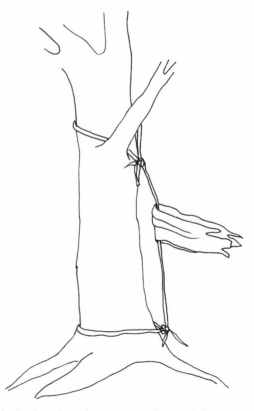 the hide together. By pulling, you break the bond in this setting glue and the hide remains soft. On a hot, dry, windy day, it will take 3 to 4 hours to soften the hide, pulling and working the hide about every 15 minutes for a 3-minute period. Then for the next two days, pull and work the neck and tail areas for about 1 minute 2 or 3 times a day. This way, there isn't any hidden dampness to stiffen up later. To keep it soft, it will need to be finished by smoking. More on this later.

Brain tanning. If the animal is not a raccoon, allow the fleshed hide to dry completely. Then lightly scrape the flesh side of the hide with a knife to rough up the hide and remove any remaining membrane.

Cook the brains with water in a ratio of about a pound of brains to a gallon of water. You'll need enough solution to cover the flesh side of the hide three times. For a coyote, we use two or three cups of water and one coyote brain. (The brain could be from any source.) To kill any bacteria, cook the brains until they turn gray. Cool them to lukewarm. Rub a third of the brain into the hide. When it has been pulverized by rubbing, add one third of the water to the hide and rub this in. Treat only the flesh side of the hide.

Let the hide dry in a cool place, out of the sun so the brain solution has a chance to penetrate. When it is dry, lightly scrape the flesh side again with a knife or hide scraper. Rub in the next third of the brains and water. Let dry and scrape as before. Brain the third time, and this time instead of letting the hide dry, put wet leaves, rags, or towels on the flesh side of the hide to prevent it from drying. Allow the hide to fully hydrate until it is wet like it was after you skinned the animal.

Now hang it to dry until it starts to turn yellow, and work dry over a rope or cable as with a raccoon hide. The head, neck, and tail will take the longest to dry. As a measure of drying time, we live in an extremely dry area and a bear neck took five days to fully hydrate and another five days to dry. It was that thick. The last two days, we only pulled it twice each day for about five minutes over a cable. Raccoon necks and tails frequently take three days to completely dry. So make sure you give them a pull now and then so they stay soft, even after you think they are dry. If you are unable to work the hide while it is drying, put it in a plastic bag and freeze it. Then thaw and work it when you can.

If some parts are still a little stiff, carefully work these by putting an axe in a vice and pulling them back and forth over this edge in the same kind of motion as shining shoes.

To tan a deer-size animal or larger with the hair on, it is helpful to lace the hide tightly to a frame after fleshing and allow it to dry. Scrape, brain, and dry at least five times, as opposed to three times for furs, before covering with wet leaves or towels.

When the hide is saturated, work by poking with a blunt object, such as a broom handle, until soft and dry. The hide should be strung loosely to the frame so it can stretch back and forth. Rotate the frame 90 degrees every 10 minutes so the top of the hide can relax.

If a hide turns out stiffer than you want, proceed to smoke it, and then rebrain. The smoke will penetrate the hide and it will soften much more easily than just rebraining without smoking.

SMOKING FURS

When the hide is dry, smoke it. Once the hide has been smoked, it can get wet without having to be completely reworked as before; a small amount of pulling will soften it again. Smoking also helps to repel insects, such as wool moths, that would ruin the fur. We often smoke our furs while we are smoking deer hides for buckskin by suspending the furs inside the bag made from buckskin. (See smoking buckskin later in this chapter.)

Another way of smoking a fur is to put it flesh-side down over a stovepipe. Have a bed of coals going in the stove and cover them with rotten wood. (The rotten wood gives off the smoke.) The stovepipe should not be so hot that you cannot hold your hand on it or you will burn the hide. For even smoking, shift the hide over the pipe opening every few minutes. Smoke until the flesh side is golden. The more you smoke it, the easier it will be to re-soften if it gets wet.

Once your fur is smoked, we recommend washing it or hanging it outside for a while to dissipate the smoky smell. If you choose to wash it, do so in cold water with a nondetergent soap. Alternatively, almost any bar hand soap will do. Rework the fur while it is drying, but you won't need to do this as often or as intensely as in the initial tanning.

MAKING RAWHIDE AND BUCKSKIN

Rawhide is untanned hide, stiff and firm. Its best uses are for rattles, drums, lashing, knife sheaths, and containers and such. **Buckskin** is chamois-soft leather, best used for clothing, shoes, and blankets.

Dehairing Method 1

Choose hides of deer, antelope, or goat. (Larger hides such as buffalo, cow, and elk are best dehaired when stretched on a frame as described in dehairing method two.)

Flesh the hide on a beam as previously described for furs. Then turn the hide over so the hair side is up. Start with the neck between the tree and the beam. With a bone scraper or dull drawknife, scrape the hair and the grain off. If you are just wanting to make rawhide, leave the grain on; just get the hair off. The grain has a smooth surface. The inner hide, the part you want for buckskin, looks a little rougher.

If you're having difficulty removing the hair, soak the hide in water for a day or two or until the hair can be pulled out, and then try it again. (Don't dehair by plucking! This is just a test to see if it's ready to dehair on the beam.) Make sure that no dirt, sand, or other foreign matter gets between the hide and the beam to make bumps in the hide that even a bone scraper can cut or tear through.

It is easiest to work in the direction the hair grows (from neck to tail). The neck area is the most difficult to work and may require additional soaking. As the hide dries, it will also be harder to work, so put it back in the bucket of water for a few minutes if it is drying. You should change the water daily to prevent bacteria from building up.

Once the hair is off, you have rawhide. If rawhide is what you want, use it now, or dry it for later use by cutting holes 1/2 inch from the edges and staking it out on the ground to dry. This way it will dry flat and you will be able to see what you have instead of a wrinkled-up piece. To use, just soak in water to soften.

To make buckskin, once the grain is removed, put the hide back in the water for a few minutes and then put it back on the beam with the flesh side up. Now scrape off the membrane on this side with your bone tool or drawknife. You will know when you have it off because there won't be any of the membrane sluffing off at the bottom of your working tool. Once the membrane and the grain are off, hang the hide out to dry. Remember, the membrane is on the flesh side of the hide, and the grain is on the hair side.

When it is dry, cook the brains in water—a pound of brains to a gallon of water. A deer has around 1/3 pound of brains, so use 1/3 gallon of water. Cook them until they are gray; then cool them until you can hold your hand in the water. Rub the brain into the dried hide to pulverize the brain. (If you don't have any brains to use on the hide, you can substitute a dozen raw eggs for a pound of brains. Just whisk them in the water, and the rest of the procedure is the same as with brains. Four or five eggs will tan a deer hide. Thanks to Steve Edelholm for this tip.) Whether you have used brains or eggs, next stuff the hide into the bucket. It will probably take a couple of hours for the stiff hide to relax enough to squish down and be completely covered by the brain water solution. If you don't have enough solution to cover the hide, add a little water.

Soak the hide until it is completely limp. You may have to unroll the edges and pull out wrinkles to get them to absorb the solution faster. Once it is all soft with no hard spots, drape the hide over a horizontal pole. Make sure the bucket is underneath; you want to save all the solution because you're not finished with it yet. This pole can be a shovel lashed to tree branches. (When we do this on canoe trips, we have someone hold a canoe paddle at chest height.) Wring out the moisture by grasping the hide at the top where it goes around the pole and pulling downward. This initial wringing will render the hide less slippery, making the next step easier.

Spread out the hide and arrange it so 1/3 of the length is hanging over one side of the pole and 2/3 is hanging over the other side. Pull the longer end around and up, overlapping the shorter end, and then back down over the pole. (The hide should look like one of those cloth towels that goes round and round in the public restroom.) Starting at one side, roll the hide up like a shirtsleeve until it looks like an oblong doughnut. Put a smooth stick 2 feet long and 2 inches in diameter in the bottom of this doughnut. Twist the stick so it winds up the hide, forcing more of the solution through the hide. Be careful, because if you use too much pressure, you can tear or blow holes in the hide. Just wring it until you see solution being forced through, and hold it there for a few seconds. Now unwind the stick, rotate the hide doughnut a quarter turn, and wind the stick up in the other direction. Wring it four times, turning the doughnut a quarter turn each time until you have gone clear around the hide. Then unroll the doughnut, pull out the wrinkles, and stick the hide back in the brains. Keep it there 10 minutes and then put it through the wringing process again using the same procedure.

When you get used to this process, you'll be able to do it in a few minutes. Remember, if your doughnut shape pulls apart as you start to wring,

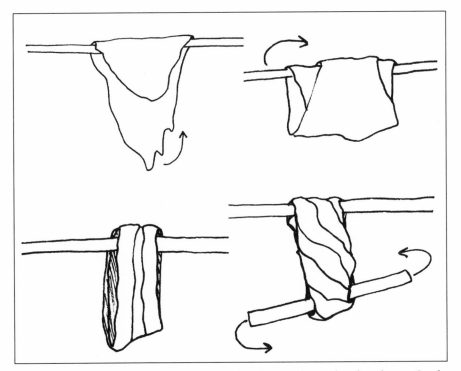

you haven't squeezed out enough liquid before making the doughnut. So do it again.

Each of these soakings and four quarter-turn wringings is called one braining. Brain deer and hides of similar thickness a minimum of 5 times (20 quarter turns spread between 5 soakings). We brain elk 10 times. If all this wringing and soaking seems like a hassle, be aware it is much easier than having the hide go stiff while working it because it didn't get enough brains, and having to start over.

After the final wringing, **sew up any holes.** If you are using a bone awl and sinew, start right away, as it will take a while and you want to finish before the hide stiffens. Make sure the stitching is tight. We use a running stitch on the flesh side. The hide will shrink and the stitching will consequently loosen, so pull a little pucker in the stitching to compensate for this. If using a glover's needle (available at leather supply stores), it is better to wait a while before sewing. Wait until the hide is turning yellow in places and then pull these stiffening spots on the rope, first one direction and then at right angles. Then start sewing. The hide will start to stiffen, so in between sewing holes pull the hide over the rope. Don't waste any time working sopping wet parts. The glue is not setting up there yet. Just focus on the parts that are getting stiff.

The edges, except for the neck, will dry the fastest. Work these first by pulling the edges back and forth over the rope. Then pull back and forth with one hand on the edge and the other in the center of the hide. This way the fibers will get worked evenly. Once you have gone around the edges, start at the neck and work to the tail; then go from one side to the next. This systematic working of the hide, first from one direction and then 90 degrees from the other direction, will prevent the fibers from gluing together.

When a part of the hide bounces back as you pull it, that part is done, even though it may be a little damp. So focus on places that still stretch without bouncing back. A section on each rump and the neck will take the longest to dry. At any time before the rump and neck are the last places left to finish, you can throw the hide into a bag and put it in the freezer to work on later. If the hide is almost dry though, the dry parts will suck up the moisture from the wet parts and the hide will be stiff at the neck and the rump even though you bagged it. So when you are that close to being finished, with only the neck and rump left to dry, stick with it or call for help. Bagging it at this point means a stiff hide.

Often the edges come out stiff for an inch in places. We trim this before smoking, as the stiff edges are hard to sew through. If your hide is stiff in places, you have several options. You could rebrain it and rework it. This second working will be quite a bit easier than the first but still a chore. Another option is to use damp wood and smoke the stiff hide. This allows the stiff spots to relax so smoke can get through. On slightly stiff or papery antelope hides, this damp smoke usually gets rid of the problem. If the hide is still stiff after smoking, then rebrain it once and rework only the stiff spots. This second working will be easy. You will only have to pull it at most a third of the amount. When you rework a smoked and rebrained hide, most of the time the hide is just hanging there drying. About every fifteen minutes, pick it up and pull it a minute or so; then hang it back to dry some more.

You must resmoke this hide after reworking to penetrate the stiff spots and finish the tanning process. Otherwise, when these unsmoked spots get wet from rain or washing, they will stiffen.

One more option with hides that have stiff spots is to adjust your clothing pattern on the hide to miss these spots.

Brain-tanned buckskin is soft like chamois, not cold and clammy like commercially tanned leathers. When the hide begins to dry and soften, the feel of it is a delightful fulfillment for the tactile senses. Softening a hide, while being a bit of work, is extremely pleasurable. You will want to squeeze it, rub it against your skin, and show it to your friends. It is a rewarding project.

Dehairing Method 2

This method uses a frame to aid in dehairing large hides. The hair and grain are cut off by scraping when the hide is dry and rigid, resulting in a hide that is thinner and fluffier, ideal for clothing. (See Chapter 3 on tools for frame building.)

To remove the hair, lay the hide on the ground, flesh side up. Punch holes every 2 inches or so, 1/2 inch from the edges. You can either stake the hide on the ground or lay a frame around the hide, and using strong cord, lace the hide to the frame. If you use the frame, tie a cord to each leg and tie the legs to the corners of the frame, first centering the hide. Lace all the way around, keeping the hide centered.

Now stand the frame up and, using the dry scraping tool described in Chapter 3 on tools, scrape the flesh off the hide. The hide will stretch a bit here, and you will need to tighten the cords or stakes.

Once the flesh is off, let the hide dry completely. Now turn the hide over and, with a sharp blade in your scraper, scrape off the hair and the grain. (If you're just after rawhide, don't worry about removing the grain. The grain often looks gray like pepper.) It's easy to scrape away too much of the hide. When in doubt, leave it on; you can always remove it later, but you can't put it back on. Places to watch out for are thin spots on the belly, the bottom of the rump, and under the front legs. It's easy to pop through these spots with a scraper. Sometimes you will get washboard bumps as you scrape. Remove these by scraping at right angles from the direction that you were moving when you made the bumps. It is better, though, not to make them at all. If the hide is dry and the blade sharp, it will be easier to avoid making these washboards.

When we use stone to scrape the hides, one blade usually stays sharp enough for one square foot of hide. We go through ten blades for a deer hide. When using steel blades, we resharpen at least once for a deer.

The membrane on the flesh side can be removed with the same scraping tool. However, it is easier to remove the membrane when the hide is brained and on the fleshing beam, as described in the first method.

Once the hair and grain have been removed, take the hide from the frame and brain it as previously described. After the first wringing, put it on the beam and scrape off the membrane. Then continue soaking and wring-ing as before. When you are done with the brains, finish the hide as in the first method.

If it is an elk or other large hide, lace it to the frame after the last wring-ing. Work it on the frame with a blunt object. When the hide has lost most of its moisture, test it by pushing in on a spot. If it stays pushed in and then slowly returns, take it off the frame. Finish working it on the rope.

Smoking the hide will finish the tanning process. In paleo days, people who had open fires in their homes merely had to suspend the hides for a week or so high above the fire. We have a woodstove set up where we smoke most of our hides.

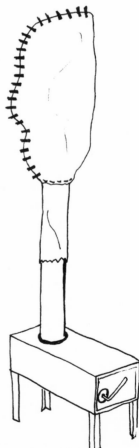

You can smoke one hide at a time by folding the hide in half and clipping or sewing the edges together. (See Chapter 3 on tools for how to make twig clips.) Or sew two or three hides together to form a big bag. Leave a 6-inch opening or so at the neck and attach a tube made of canvas or an old denim pant leg at the opening. Make the cloth tube 2 feet long. Then start a hardwood or charcoal fire in the stove. When there is a good bed of coals, add rotten wood to make smoke. Our favorite is dry, pulverized cottonwood from a rotting hollow log.

Suspend the hide with the cloth tube attached over the stove, and put the tube over the stovepipe. To be safe, place the hide a couple of feet above the stove to keep it from scorching. Even with this distance, the fire should be low enough that there are no big flames in the stove and you can place your hand on the pipe without burning it. Pin strings to the sides of the hide and pull it out so the smoke can get everywhere. When smoke color comes through the thicker portions of the hide and it is golden brown, turn the hide bag inside out and smoke the other side until the colors match.

Another way to smoke the hide is to dig a hole in the ground 1 foot or deeper. The diameter of the hole should be a little smaller than the opening in the hide bag. Push a stick 1 inch in diameter into the ground a foot away from the hole, angling into the bottom of the hole to create an air intake. Without this intake the fire will suffocate. Now remove the stick and build a fire in the hole. When it has turned to coals, add the rotten wood. Suspend the hide over the hole. Seal the edges of the bag around the hole with sand or dry dirt and smoke as before. A small cloth or leather tube connected to the opening in the hide is helpful, as the bottom edge of the hide will not get well smoked because it is covered in dirt.

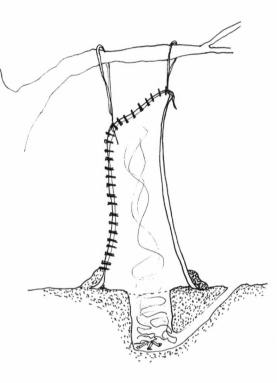

The hides will smell very smoky. If you want to make clothes from them, wash them first. Soak them in cool water and mild *non-detergent* soap for a couple of hours. Rinse, wring, and hang out to dry. When dry, pull them a minute or so over the rope to restore their original softness. You will find that the hides have shrunk a little. For this reason, as well as the intensity of the odor, we recommend washing all your smoked hides before making garments.

With all the potential items animals offer—from food to clothing, rawhide lacing to shelter, containers to music—we can be thankful for the tremendous gifts they bestow.

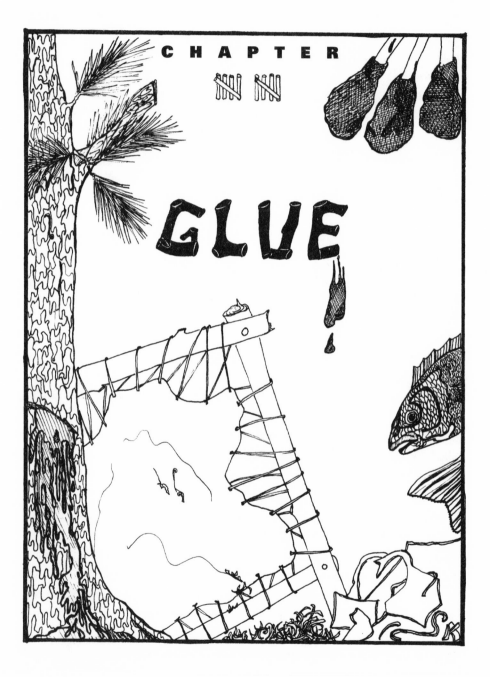

CHAPTER

GLUE

HARDLY A WEEK GOES BY WHERE REPAIRS OR PROJECTS don't have most of us reaching for that hot-glue gun or a bottle of Elmer's. Local resources offer some great natural alternatives to store-bought glues. These glues are strong and can be completely nontoxic.

PITCH GLUE

Let's start with pitch glue. Pitch glue is nature's hot glue, and it's waterproof, too. Pitch is the sticky resin that drips from gashes or branch breaks on coniferous trees. Any pine, fir, or spruce will bleed pitch.

Pitch glue is about twice as strong as commercial contact cement and has many applications, including filling cracks in wooden bowls, attaching arrowheads to arrow shafts, coating basketry to make waterproof containers, repairing shoe and boot seams temporarily to keep out water, and numerous craft applications. You get a bonus using pitch to glue crafty Christmas decorations because the glue has a great pine aroma. Don't forget other potpourri possibilities, knife-blade hafting (see Chapter 3 on tools for more details), clay pot repairs, paper projects (keep it very runny), and, when mixed with alcohol, pitch makes an excellent varnish (see further in this chapter).

GATHERING PITCH

First, gather the pitch. Including as little dirt and debris as possible along with the pitch is a goal to aim for, but when you melt the pitch, any impurities can be skimmed off.

Carry some extra paper sacks and a pocketknife on any hike or outing. You'll usually come across pitch at some point or other. Fresh pitch is very sticky but easier to gather than hardened pitch; however, it clings to the knife blade. Wiping the knife on the inside of the paper bag helps clean the pitch from the blade.

If you find dried pitch, hack at the hardened drops with the knife, moving the blade in a skimming, downward angle that doesn't remove underlying bark. Hold the bag under the area you are working so the pitch falls into the bag. This keeps the pitch from sticking to pine needles, dirt, and leaves on the ground. However, as you hack away, bits of pitch go flying all over, so go ahead and pick up what falls on the ground, too. Once you have collected the pitch, you are ready to make glue.

Making Pitch Glue. Choose a smallish cooking container such as a clay pot, old kitchen pot, or tin can with the lid removed. Small batches are best because overcooking yields too brittle a glue, and you have to keep the pitch hot while applying. It heats very quickly so small batches are no inconvenience.

Heat the pitch gently until it liquefies. Then, either dip a stick into the liquid pitch and apply with this stick, or pour the pitch directly onto what you are gluing. The sticks, bark, dirt, etc., can remain in the can. If some debris does get on the glued surface, just pick it off.

However, being potless does not present a problem for the paleo proficient. Simply set a flat rock (flat, so the melting pitch doesn't run off the sides of the rock) close to the fire and put the pitch on the rock. As the pitch melts you can scoop it up with a stick and apply it. Another potless method is to mold a glob of raw pitch onto the end of a stick and hold this near the heat. Be careful, because pitch is very flammable. This is okay if you need the glue more solid, but with too much flaming the glue will become brittle and of poorer quality. So, find the right distance from the fire, and as the pitch begins to melt, let the drops fall onto the item you want to glue.

Other Uses of Pitch. Besides glue, pitch can be used as a bug deterrent and as an antiseptic. To use pitch as a bug deterrent, simply melt some in the bottom of a can. Shake in a generous amount of black pepper (gesundheit!), and heat the pitch-pepper mix until it begins to smoke. Take the smoking can to your doorways and windows and let the smoke coat the sills, jambs, and screens (especially where the holes are). Do this on your porch area as well, in the barn, or wherever to help reduce house flies and gnats. This same process done with dried and crushed tansy instead of pepper will help repel biting flies. As an antiseptic, pitch works well on small cuts and nicks because of the turpines in the resin. Hold a little pitch between your thumb and finger until it warms and softens. Rub the pitch on the injured area.

HIDE GLUE

Hide glue is almost four times stronger than airplane cement and a third stronger than five-minute epoxy.* It is easy to make and simple to preserve. You need to cook raw, untanned hide in water to make this glue.

Finding and Preparing the Hide. There are many resources for finding rawhide. Butchers who process whole animals are usually happy to sell you a hide. Drum makers often have more scrap than they can use. Taxidermists, tanneries, saddle makers, and other leather goods producers usually have rawhide to sell or in scrap form for free. Friends who hunt are another source.

*Research by Tim Baker.

Of course, if you are already tanning hides, you have your glue source at hand! Just save all the little scrapings of epidermis and membrane as well as any edges you pull or trim off. Also, sinew scraps can be saved and thrown into the pot.

With all these options there is no need to steal Fido's rawhide pull toy! However, rawhide sold in pet stores is also viable. Just soak the rawhide dough-nut in water until it is soft (this may take several days), and then unroll it.

If you obtain raw, untanned hides with the hair still on, you'll want to scrape the hair off (see Chapter 9 on animals) before cutting up scraps to cook into glue. You can cook hide pieces with the hair still on, but this busi-ness of straining out the hair afterwards is a real mess and time consuming.

Once you have obtained a hide, cut it into very little pieces. This allows for quicker extraction of the protein (which makes the glue) and lower cook-ing temperature (which keeps the final product stronger).

Extracting the Glue. Before you start cooking the glue, here's some advice: plug in a burner on the back porch or in the backyard, or prepare a cook fire in the back forty, downwind of open windows. The cooking glue is extremely odoriferous in an earthy sort of way, and cooking outside will mini-mize complaints from your household companions.

1. Toss all the little scraps of hide into a large pot (a clay pot or #10 can works great and saves kitchen arguments) and cover with water. If you have tiny hide shavings that will cook faster, save these and add to the pot for the last two hours of cooking.

2. Bring the water temperature up to 140 degrees, but don't let it exceed 180. How do you do this without a thermometer? First, keep it from boiling; it should be slightly steaming if the surrounding air is 65 or above. (If it's cold outside, there will be more steam than if the air is warm.) Otherwise use a thermometer, as high temperature will really weaken the glue.

Keep the glue cooking in this temperature range for 12 to 24 hours, until all the scraps have swollen and become gelatinous, releasing their protein. (If only shavings are being used, a couple hours will be enough cooking time.)

3. Cool the liquid just enough to prevent burns when handling it.

4. Pour this mixture into a thin linen dish towel or cheesecloth, and squeeze out the watery glue, leaving the scraps in the towel.

5. The scraps can be placed back in another pot, covered with water, and a second extraction of glue can be made. This second extraction is a little weaker, but you probably won't notice. With the second extraction, just cook

it another hour and then strain as before. Then cook the watery glue down some more, at 140 degrees, without the scraps, until it is like runny syrup.

Using the Hide Glue. Now you're ready to glue something. The glue should be cooled to hot bathwater temperature when you're using it. If the glue cools too much, it becomes gelatinous and won't work as well. If it does jell, simply bring up the temperature, but the more you jell and reliquefy, the weaker the glue will become.

If you are gluing wood surfaces, first clean the surface with a little soap and water. (An optional cleaner is a weak lye solution made by pouring water through wood ashes and saving this strained water to wash the wood surfaces.) Rinse off the soap, then coat the surfaces with glue and allow some glue to soak into the wood. After this first coating of glue has had a chance to soak in for a minute, recoat the surfaces and clamp them together.

Hide glue works best where a tight fit is wanted. If the gluing process is prolonged, you may need to periodically add more water to the glue pot, keeping the glue at a proper consistency. Allow a few days drying time for jobs requiring strength, or even longer time in humid climates.

The good news is that hide glue is water soluble. So if you've used kitchen towels and pots that someone is upset about, your reproachable behavior is now redeemable. Still, it's beneficial to your well-being to set aside your own set of "project" tools that don't have to do double duty in the kitchen. Water solubility, however, is not always desired. Waterproofing of glued areas can be done by sealing the glued seams with fat, oil, or a varnish made from crushed pitch and rubbing alcohol. Simply dissolve the pitch in the alcohol in a ratio of about four parts alcohol to one part pitch. Several light coats work best.

FISH SKIN GLUE

Another way to get glue material is to use fish skins and bladders. Fish bladder is strong like hide glue and jells. If you fish, you're all set. Otherwise, go to the fish market where they prepare fillets and other cuts. This glue preparation is the same as for hide glue and also offers an invigorating nasal experience!

STORING AND REUSING LEFTOVER GLUE

So, now you've made up some glue, glued something, and have a pot of glue left over. What to do? If it's pitch glue and you've wisely designated a can for this purpose, leave it in the can and reheat it when you need it.

If it's hide or fish glue, it must be completely dried to prevent rotting. Cook the glue down to a very thick mass, being careful to prevent scorching. Pour the glue onto a cookie sheet in as thin a layer as possible and let it dry. In dry climates this happens quickly, and a hot sun speeds the process. If the weather is damp and overcast, you'll need another heat source to aid drying (a very low oven, a food dehydrator, heat lamp, woodstove, etc.). Do not use a glass dish to dry the glue. The glue is so strong, it may rip chunks of glass away from the dish as it dries.

As the hide glue dries, it forms a hard jell. Fish skin glue dries until it is like leather. During the process, cut this jell or leather into quarter-inch chunks to aid drying. When it is rock hard, it can be stored indefinitely.

For the most convenient reconstituting, grind these chunks into a powder between two rocks. (Or grind them in a blender. In a blender the glue, as well as rubber parts, can get very hot, so go easy and do small batches to avoid ruining your seals and bearings.) Store the powdered glue in moisture-proof containers. When you're ready to glue again, add two parts water to one part crystals, soak half an hour, and heat.

Making glue sticks is another storage technique that works well. As the pitch or hide glue cools, twirl a small twig around in the glue until it looks like a giant Q-Tip. This may take several applications, letting the glue set and redipping it. Poke the unglued end of the stick into the ground and allow the glue to harden. (If it's hide glue, keep it in the shade and away from a fire at first or it will melt and run off the stick.)

For pitch glue sticks, just heat the pitch and use. For hide glue sticks, wet the glue stick repeatedly until a layer of gel forms on the outside of the glue glob. Heat this jell till it liquefies and apply.

Knox unflavored gelatin is a commercial version of this versatile glue. We use Knox when we run out of hide glue. Many desserts and store-bought yogurts have gelatin in them. So if you really get in a pinch, remember, your hide glue is edible, as long as you've used hides that weren't rotten. As a matter of fact, we once accidentally added some powdered hide glue to some spaghetti sauce on a camp-out. It had been conveniently placed in a clear film container and stuck in the camp spice ditty bag. We thought it was sugar-in-the-raw! Mmm, mmm, good!

So there you have some glues that you can make yourself and that work as well as or better than commercial options. And you won't have to call the poison control center if you find Junior with his face in the glue pot.

Go ahead and pull out those repairs and projects you've been procrastinating and get them all stuck together.

CHAPTER

MUSIC

MUSIC HAS PLAYED AN IMPORTANT ROLE IN ALL AGES of humankind. It lifts the spirit, warms the heart, and is food for the soul. Hand on hand, stick on stick, and rock on rock may have been the first instruments we learned to use. They worked well then and still work now. It's amazing what kind of a great rhythm jam you can get going between a small group of folks clapping and beating sticks and stones.

Hard, dense wood seems to give the clearest sound. The same goes for stone, the harder the better. Quartzite, granite, and basalt work well.

STICK PERCUSSION INSTRUMENT

You could simply beat two sticks together to create rhythm. Or, by refining the stick to get more than a pounding sound, you can come up with great audio variety.

Cutting a series of notches down the length of a stick or antler (like a washboard) turns it into one of our favorite percussion instruments. We call our notched stick a reet reet. Scrape a stick, shell, bone, piece of gourd, or chip of stone up and down the notched stick. It makes a rapid clinking sound that almost becomes a chirp when done quickly. Reet! Reet!

Experiment with several sticks to see what difference the distance between notches makes, and also the depth of notches. If the notches are close together, your stick instrument could mimic the Latin American *guiro*, which is a serrated gourd played by rubbing a stick up and down its length.

RAIN STICK

Rain sticks are easy if you have some material that can quickly be made into a tube. Reeds, cholla cactus, bamboo, and agave will work. Hollow the center, leaving one end sealed. Drill little holes all around the sides of the column and insert thorns or slivers of wood through the holes that extend well inside the cavity, even all the way across. Glue them in place with hide glue (see Chapter 10 on glue). Put in some rice, seeds, or tiny stones. Then seal off the end with a glued wooden plug. Invert and listen to the rain.

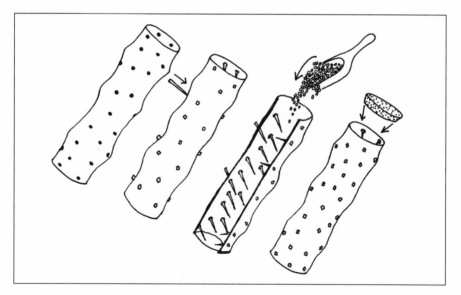

STICK RATTLE

You will need a stick with forked branches at the ends to hold the rattle pieces. Peel and whittle the stick until it has a fairly smooth surface.

Cut slices (round discs) of gourd or wood; then drill a hole in the center of each disc big enough to fit over the stick. The forked end keeps the discs from falling off the one side. Make sure the hole in each disk is large enough so the disks slide freely up and down the stick. After all the discs have been skewered, wrap cord around the unforked end to form a lump that will keep the discs from sliding off. Then shake away. See how many different sounds you can create from your instruments, and experiment to adjust the rhythm.

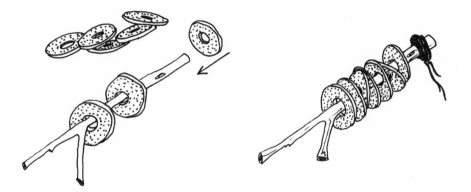

RAWHIDE RATTLE

It's fun to make a rawhide rattle—any shape or size will do. You will need enough rawhide to cut two pieces the same size and shape, plus enough rawhide lacing to lace the two pieces together all around the outside edges. And you'll need a stick for a handle and something "rattley" to put inside. After your rattle is finished, you can decorate it with paint if you like. Just follow these steps:

1. Soak the rawhide until it is limp.

2. Decide what shape you want to make your rattle; it could be round like a balloon or shaped like some animal. Cut two pieces the same shape and size. Leave a 1-inch lip at the base of your shape where the stick handle will go; this is the piece of material you will lash onto the handle.

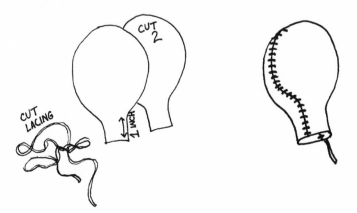

3. Sew the two pieces of wet rawhide together tightly with wet rawhide lacing or wet sinew, leaving the bottom open. Both lacing and sinew will shrink as the rawhide dries and shrinks, so the seam will remain tight.

4. Put as much dry sand in the hole as possible, pushing out the rawhide to its full dimensional shape. Insert a stick where you have left a space for the handle. Temporarily lash the rawhide to the stick. Set aside to dry.

5. Once it is dry, remove the lashing and the stick and shake out the sand. Insert some small pebbles, popcorn, or seeds. You don't need many to get a satisfying sound. Put the stick back in and bind the rattle to the stick with wet rawhide.

6. Decorate the rattle with paints, if you like, to make yours unique. Use paints you make yourself (see Chapter 4 on color).

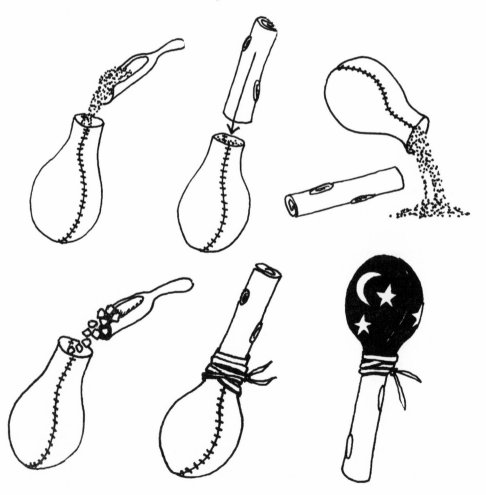

TAMBOURINE

You can make a tambourine by either stringing shells or suspending them from a hoop.

To make a string tambourine, gather seashells. Worms often eat into clams and other shells, leaving tiny holes. If you have shells without holes, you can drill small ones. (See Chapter 3 on tools for how to make a drill.) Shell is brittle, so be careful not to use too much pressure.

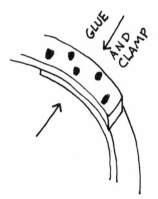

String the shells and then suspend the string rather tightly between two branches or between the two sides of a forked stick. Shake away!

To make a hoop tambourine:

1. Make a hoop with a thin wood slat that has been beveled at an angle on each end. The angles should be opposite each other for neatness. If the wood is green and pliable, slowly bend the slat into a circular shape. (If the wood is dry, steam the slat for 30 minutes over a pot of boiling water before you try bending it.) Make sure the ends overlap at least 4 inches. This will keep the hoop from twisting.

2. Clamp to shape using a tourniquet-like clamp. (See Chapter 3 on tools.) Allow the slat to dry.

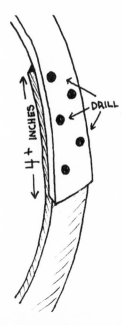

3. Drill a few holes through both layers for rawhide lacing. Then use hide glue (see Chapter 10) to glue the two ends of wood together. Then lace the holes with wet rawhide to secure the glued ends of the hoop.

4. Drill an even number of holes around one edge for attaching the shells. String a piece of lacing through each two holes. Lace from the outside to the inside and back to the outside. Tie an overhand knot against the hoop on each lacing end so the lacing doesn't slip around. Now tie a shell to each lacing end.

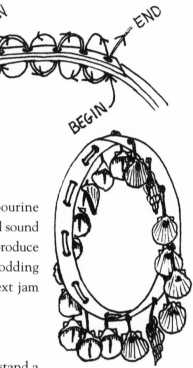

This tambourine makes a beautiful sound and is sure to produce smiles and nodding heads in your next jam session.

DRUM

Making drums is easy once you understand a few principles. First, the idea is to stretch a piece of wet rawhide over a round frame or hoop and let it dry. Second, the frame base must have a rounded, level edge where the hide will be stretched over the edge. If this edge is flat or uneven, the drum will buzz. Third, the hoop base must be sturdy. If it is weak, it will warp as the rawhide dries and shrinks.

Drums may wrinkle in humid conditions. Just warm them by the fire or stove before playing and the wrinkles will disappear. Be careful not to burn the skin. As the drum skin warms, the pitch of the drum will go up. You can put rendered fat on the drum skin to make it water repellent. Natural paints look great on drums too! (See Chapter 4 on color.)

Log-Frame Drum. Drums can be made with hollowed-out logs.

1. Find a log that already has a hole in it (many do). A width of about 8 to 10 inches is a good size for this kind of drum. Saw off the desired length.

About 12 inches is adequate.

2. Use antler or wood wedges to en-large the hole until the walls are an inch or less thick. You may want to reinforce the log from the outside with a rope wrapped around and around to keep the walls from splitting while you are doing this.

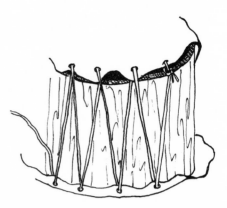

3. Once the log is hollow, flatten the edges on each end by grinding on a side-walk or flat rock. You want the drum edges level. Then round the edges by further grinding, rasping, or sanding. If you want a drum skin on both ends of the drum, round both ends.

4. It's a good idea to then waterproof the wood where the wet hide will touch it. If the wood gets wet, it will dry slowly and shrink *after* the rawhide has dried and shrunk. This will leave you with a bad-sounding drum. So, rub the edges with wax or rendered fat until they are well coated.

5. Now, soak some rawhide in water until it is totally pliable and stretchy.

6. Lay out the rawhide on a clean surface and set the drum base on it. Using a piece of charcoal, sketch out the circle you want to cut. Cut a drum skin that overlaps your drum base by at least 1 inch. (An obsidian edge works great for cutting. See Chapter 3 on tools.) The hide will stretch as you lace it up, but if you cut it too small, you're out of luck! For this log-frame drum, you may want two drum skins; if so, cut two the same size. Then lace the drum as in the picture above.

7. Punch out holes around the edges of the skin for the lacing. This isn't rocket science, so just punch holes. For a 10-inch drum base you'll want approximately 20 holes spaced as evenly as possible. Keep them from getting too close to the edge as they might rip through when you tighten your laces.

Opt. A

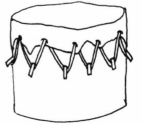

Opt. B

If you're doing two, do the same number of holes in each skin.

8. Cut lacing that has a consistent thickness. You'll need about 2 yards for this 1-foot log-frame drum. Follow the drawing for lacing the log-frame drum, either option A or B on page 171.

9. Do not play the drum at all until it has dried thoroughly.

Hoop-Frame Drums. Gourds can be used for drum hoop bases, but be careful not to lace the hide too tightly or the gourd will crush.

You can also split wood and thin it to an eighth of an inch or less; then steam and bend into a hoop. Follow the same process as with the tambourine hoop. For a drum hoop, it is better to double the length of the wood slat and go around twice. (A 10-inch hoop is a good size.) This makes it more sturdy and less likely to warp. Make sure the hoop edges are level so the drum skin will be flat. Wax the edge before lacing the drum.

Cut lacing that has a consistent thickness. You'll need about 3 yards of lacing for that 10-inch drum. Lay the hoop on the hide. Cut the hide

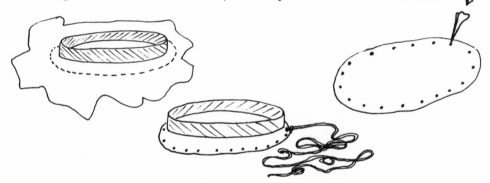

with at least a 1-inch overlap. Punch 20 holes all the way around.

Tie an end of the lacing to one of the holes (#1) you have punched. Set the hoop on the skin and run your lace through the hole directly opposite the hole you just tied on to. This second hole is labeled #2. Pull this first length of lace snug between the two holes. Tie a half hitch in the center and go perpendicular to #3.

Now thread three holes at a time at #3, return to center and make a half hitch, go across to #4, thread three holes there, return to center and make a half hitch, go to #5, etc. Always make the center half hitch after each thread-ing of holes. It will look like spokes on a wheel. If you have 20 holes and thread 3 holes each from numbers 3 to 8, you will have 8 spokes. This center of laces will make a good handhold.

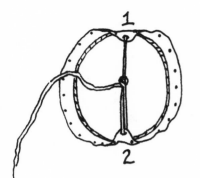 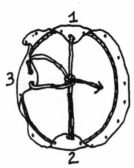

Do not play the drum at all until it has dried thoroughly.

Another way to make a drum base is with clay (see Chapter 6 on pottery). Be sure to make your pottery drum base with thick walls so it will not break as the hide dries. With low-fired clay we like to use a thin skin and string it more loosely so as not to stress the clay.

Drum Stick. Make a beater for your drum by taking a stick and a couple of pieces of soft leather. Wad up one piece of leather and put it in the center of the other piece. Lash this outer piece of leather to the drum stick with a wet piece of leather or rawhide lacing. Let it dry, then beat out a rhythm and connect with your paleo ancestors.

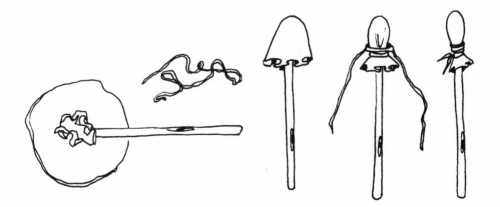

FLUTE

Consider a clay flute. It may have only a few notes, but the feelings this music evokes are powerful.

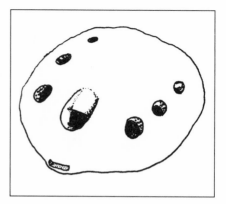

To make a clay flute, pinch a ball of clay into a hollow form. You can make the shape of the flute any shape you want, but start out with a simple round shape like the diagram. Follow the accompanying illustrations to cut a notch, blow hole, and finger holes. The notch, or angled part of clay that splits the air, should be a quarter of an inch from where the air will come out of the mouthpiece. In other words, there will be a 1/4-inch by 1/4-inch hole there.

The blow hole should be made with a flat stick 1/8 inch wide (horizontally) by just less than 1/16 inch thick. Poke this stick into the mouthpiece to make the blow hole. Angle the path of the air so that it will be split by the notch in the flute. When you look through the blow hole, all you should see is the line of the notch that splits the air. This takes a little experimenting.

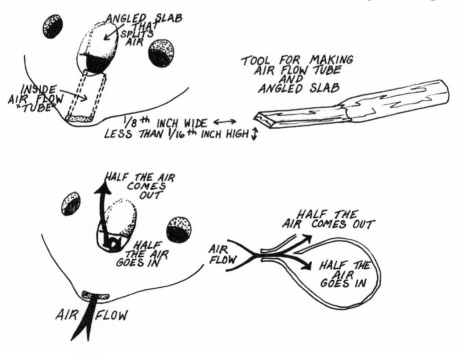

Blow each time you adjust the hole. You may have to angle the notch more or less or adjust the angle of the blow hole so that it hits the notch correctly. The far end of the blow hole must be flat and narrow, just like the dimensions of the stick used to make it.

When you get a clear tone, put in two to six finger holes, depending on sound quality. Test the tone with each new hole. Some flutes will give clear notes with more holes. Some will only tolerate two holes. Our favorite one so far only has two holes but has a scale of four notes, depending on finger position.

Let the flute dry completely and then fire it (see Chapter 6 on pottery). The flute will last longer if fired, but don't let firing stop you from making one. We have made and used many that never were fired. They just need more care to keep them from breaking and they don't look as good, but they are still wonderful music makers.

Fired or unfired, these flutes can be stylized any way your imagination works. We have flutes looking like turtles, birds, or other animals, and some like apple turnovers. Others look like things we won't mention. Still, they sound lovely.

So now you have a great variety of instruments that are fun to play and are not intimidating. Gather your friends together and make some beautiful music.

CHAPTER 11

GETTING DRESSED

IMAGINE BEING CLOTHED IN ALL-NATURAL MATERIALS that you have fashioned yourself. It's an outrageous look! This chapter has ideas that go from head to toe. And when you go out "tapping toe" dressed in these personalized garments, you'll be turning a lot of heads.

Our experimentation in making things to wear began with the simple in-and-out weaving of plant fibers, trying to come up with a good shoe sole. We made a lot of floor and wall mats this way, too. A couple of summers ago, Star showed us a sun visor she had made. It was a great idea, quick and fun to make. We hope you'll enjoy making a visor and many other items of clothing described in this chapter.

SUN VISOR

You need 20 long strips of plant fiber about 1/2 inch wide. Iris leaves, big grasses, or cattails are some things that work. They need to be flexible enough to be bent in half without ripping or breaking, and long enough to wrap twice around your head.

Collect your material and bend each of the 20 strips in half. Join the first two like this (figures 1, 2, 3, 4):

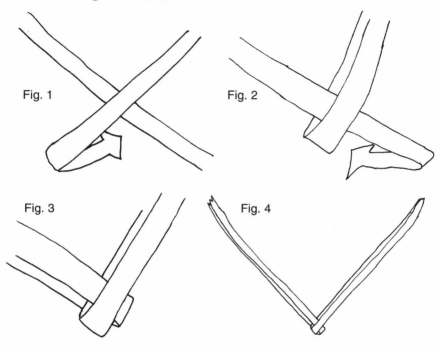

Lay them flat on the ground in front of you with the bottom of the **V** pointing at you. Add a third strip on one side of the **V** by putting the original strip in between its fold (figure 5).

Add a fourth strip to the opposite side of the **V** and lay it under the third piece (figure 6).

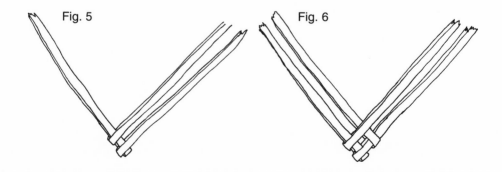

Add the fifth strip on the opposite side from the fourth and weave it under that fourth strip. Each time you add a new strip up the **V**, put the original **V** strip in between the two halves of the new addition and pull it snug to the fold of the addition. As you lay it under or begin to weave it into the other strips, keep the two folded halves of the strip together as if they were one piece (figure 7).

Add a sixth strip that goes over the third and under the fifth (figure 8).

Now you are beginning to weave. Keep adding strips to alternate sides, and weave them as far in as you can (figure 9).

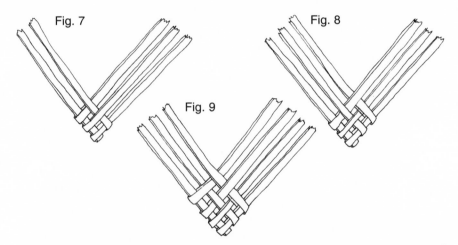

Fig. 7

Fig. 8

Fig. 9

By the time you've added all the strips, the whole front of the visor will have been woven (figure 10).

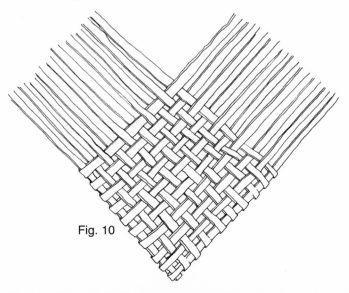

Fig. 10

To finish the brims and sides, take the last added strip of one side, bend it across to the other side in a sharp bend, and weave it down and in and out of the strip ends of that side (figure 11). When you get to the bottom of that side of ends, bend the strip back up and weave in and out to the top again (figure 12). When you get to the top, join the next strip with this original end (figure 13). Now weave down to the bottom with these joined ends. As you work down, the original end will probably run out (figure 14). Just continue down and up again with the second end, and join it to the third end when you get back to the top (figure 15). Continue this process until the edge is as long as you want it; then cord or braid the remaining ends to a finish (figures 16, 17). If the ends are not as long as you need them, tie cord or lacing to the knotted ends, and use this to fasten the visor. Now you have a great sunny weather hat.

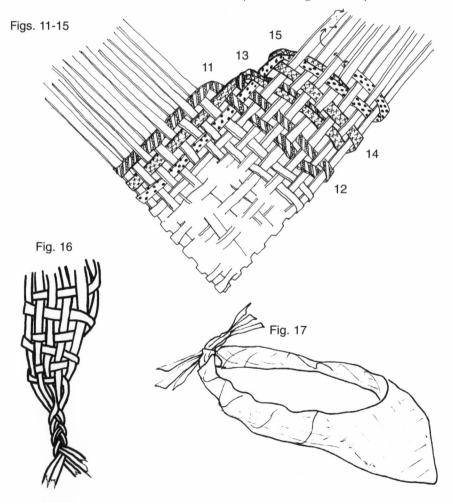

Figs. 11-15

15

13

11

14

12

Fig. 16

Fig. 17

Hints for Making and Cleaning Leather Clothing

Here are some things to keep in mind when making clothing from leather. Remember to plan your project so the hair side of the skin is facing to the outside, the flesh to the inside. The flesh side is softer against your skin. It also wears out more quickly.

If you use a pattern, always mark it out on the flesh side so the marks you make won't show on the outside of the garment. Making patterns isn't very hard. Use a piece of clothing you like for a pattern. You can trace it on to newspaper. Make up the item from an old sheet to confirm the fit and style of the final product before cutting into the leather.

There are some things to remember about leather stretch and wear as you are creating your clothing. Sleeves and legs tend to thin out and stretch longer over time, so cut them a little wider than you want them. However, don't cut them shorter because, first, this stretch doesn't show until after a few washings and, second, it doesn't always happen. Never shorten anything until you've worn it for awhile.

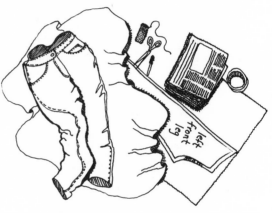

Pockets tend to droop down when they are cut on a horizontal line like a jeans design, so it's good to cut them with less curve along the pocket edge and not as far down as you would like to. They will stretch out and sit lower as you wear them. Waistbands will also loosen considerably as you wear your garments, so go ahead and fit them snugly when you start. Boot moccasins will generally stretch out along the length of the foot, so if you want to cut them roomy, add that room in the width, not the length.

Edging is a great way to put attractive borders on your clothing, and it also prevents sleeves, hems, and neck openings from stretching out and losing their shape. This is also a good idea for pocket edges. Using a darker smoked leather for the edging creates a nice look.

Leather will not lay flat like cloth. After a hide is tanned, its edges are wavy and soft. You need to work around these edges as you lay out your patterns to get the most out of your leather. This is easy to do. Adjust the pattern pieces on the leather so you have them set the way you want them. As you go to cut around the pattern pieces, push the waves in the edges out and up or down from the area you are cutting. Every 4 or 5 inches of cutting, recheck that the pattern is where you want it to be and smooth the edges again. As you cut out the pieces, the edges of the leather will flatten; these remnants can be used for collars, waistbands, cuffs, and other long thin pattern pieces. Sometimes the edges are just too wavy to work this way and you have to be really creative about getting the most from each hide. You can re-wet the hide and rack it up on a frame; then work it, stretching the waviness out of it.

This information should help you get garments made without a lot of aggravation. We sure hope it helps you avoid all the mistakes we have made over the years! Here are some stitching ideas and seam closures:

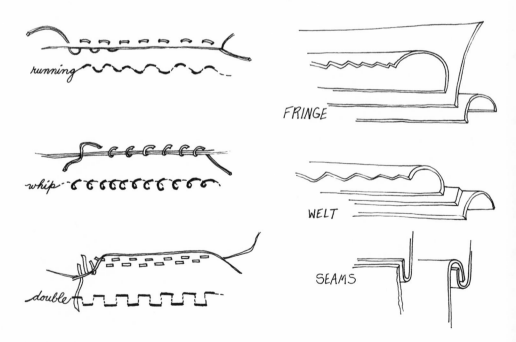

running

whip

double

FRINGE

WELT

SEAMS

Brain-tanned leather is washable! We have washed our clothes for many years and they are still soft. This may seem incredible, but when you understand what happens in the tanning, you can see why this works. In commercial tanned leather the fibers are actually broken and then softened by working oil into the leather. Once this oil is removed by washing, the leather stiffens. But brain-tanned buckskin fibers are covered with pitch from the smoking process. This waterproofs the fibers so they are protected when they get wet. When the garments dry, they are stiff like a line-dried terry towel. With just a little pulling they will soften.

Washing leather clothes in the sink is better than in the washing machine because you can feel the water temperature in the sink and won't get the water too hot. Hot water turns leather into a weird rubbery substance not fit for wearing. Also, strings and fringe and buttons won't get caught or ripped in the sink.

The best kind of soap to use is a mild one such as yucca or soapwort, or any soap you would use on your body. Whatever you choose, make sure it's *nonde-tergent* so it won't wash the pitch away. Soak the clothes for an hour in sudsy, lukewarm water. Wash the dirtier spots between your knuckles or on a wash-board after the soaking. Then rinse clean. Pull clothes into roughly the shape they were and lay out to dry. If you hang them, they will lengthen some. When they are almost dry, pull them back and forth by hand, then let them dry all the way. They will be soft. If you let them dry completely without pulling them and they feel stiff, don't fret. Pull them back and forth over a rope (gently so you don't tear the seams) for a minute or two, just as in tanning.

FUR HAT

For colder weather you may want to fashion a hat from a raccoon or other fur bearer. You will need a tanned fur, a sharp cutting edge, paper, tape, and a pencil. The first thing to remember is not to use scissors! Scissors cut the fur, and your seams will look bald. To cut out the pieces for the hat, use an obsidian blade or something similar, and always cut from the skin side.

To make a pattern for cutting the fur, you need to take four different head measurements of the person you want the hat to fit.

A) Measure around the head. Take this measurement high, about 2 inches above the eyebrows and ears. This will be the top of the hat.

B) Measure from the top headpiece line (A) to just above the eyebrows for the width of piece B. The length will be determined by pieces C and D. All these pieces together along their top edges must equal the distance around piece A. Center piece B so you get a full mask on the front of the hat.

C) Measure a width for the side band pieces C at two places. The first width is from the corner of the eye up to the top head piece line, along the edge of piece B. The second width is from the head line to the lower third of the ear. This piece has a sloping width.

D) Piece D will be the widest piece, coming down all the way to the back of the head at the tail and to below the ears behind each ear.

Once you have these measurements, you can start drawing out the pattern pieces on a piece of paper. Don't forget to cut extra allowance for seams. Tape the paper pattern pieces together and try them on to make sure they fit. Then lay the pattern on the skin side of the hide as shown, trace the pieces, and cut them out with a sharp blade from the skin side. Sew them together like the picture below.

When you sew up the seams, push all the fur away so you don't sew the fur tips

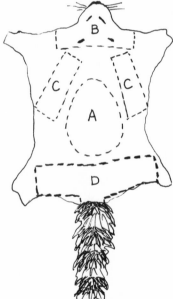

into the seam. The inside of the hat shouldn't have fur tips sticking through the seams. This will make your hat look seamless from the fur side. Use the remaining scraps to pad rough spots inside the hat that contact your skin. Let it snow!

NO-PATTERN BUCKSKIN SHIRT

The no-pattern buckskin shirt is quick and easy to make. It takes 1 1/2 large or 2 medium deer hides. You also need lacing, a bone awl, and a sharp cutting edge.

Fold one large hide, flesh side toward your skin, at the 2/3 line, letting the smaller length fall to the front to make a yoke. The back 2/3 should be long enough to give all the length you want in the back of the shirt.

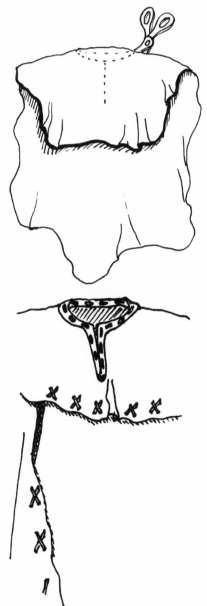

Choose a good spot for the head and neck hole and cut a circular opening. Make a slit down the center front. This slit should be edged later to prevent it from stretching out and losing its shape

Lay a second hide underneath the yoke of the first hide, flesh side down. Punch holes and lace the two pieces together in cross-stitches. Lace only across the front of the chest area, not all the way around to the sides, as this would mess up the sleeve fit later on. It takes only a few lacings to get a solid connection, and if you take your stitches intermittently, you can get them between the waves of the edge of the leather so the yoke falls gracefully.

To sew the sides together, overlap the back piece on the front piece at both sides and take 3 to 5 lacing stitches, starting at about the waist.

Now you are ready to make a slit in the back hide below the armpit so you can shape a sleeve. Most hides are wide enough to give a short sleeve to the shirt but sometimes they aren't; so if yours isn't, skip this part.

Angle the slit so that the flap of leather that hangs down from the back of the arm can be brought up and under the edge of the front yoke to form the sleeve. Just a few stitches will hold this sleeve in place. If you need to add hide to the back length, do it the same way you added hide to the front yoke piece.

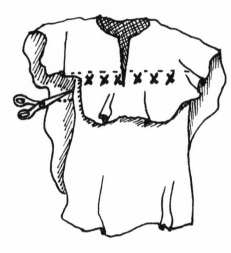 

NO-PATTERN SKIRT

This no pattern skirt takes two deer hides, lacing, buttons, and a bone awl. This skirt can be finished in a few hours, and nothing so elegant has come out of Paris in decades.

Measure the width of the hides to make sure they are wide enough to overlap several inches at the person's hips. Fold over 6 or 8 inches of the top edge of each hide to the outside, forming a somewhat triangular flap with the flesh side of the hide showing. This will become the waistband of the skirt.

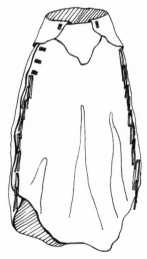

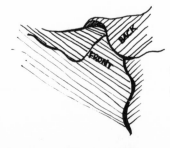

Put the folded edges of the front hide into the folds of the back hide like this:

Remember to have the flesh side toward your skin. The back looks like this:

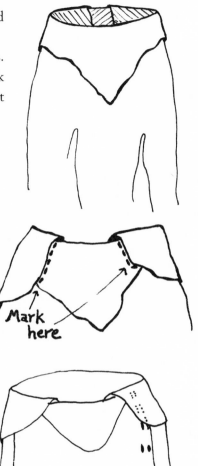

Snug up the waist and mark the side lines. The front hide edges will be over the back hide edges. Also mark where the top waist folds overlap each other.

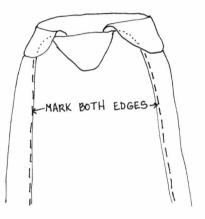

Punch sets of lacing holes. On one side, punch all the way to the top of the waistline by going underneath the first two layers of the waist fold. On the other side, stop about 4 inches from the waist flap so you can add 3 or so buttons instead of lacing. Lace all the holes. Put the side buttons in place and cut the button holes. On the side of the fold that you laced all the way, place a button on the waist fold and sew it through all four thicknesses of hide. On the side with the button opening, sew the waist fold button to the front hide only, both thicknesses. Put a button-hole in the outer part of the back waist fold.

Tuck in your shirt, put up your bone awl and lacing, and head out in style!

MAKING BUTTONS

Making buttons can be fast if you have some sort of vice (see Chapter 3 on tools), a saw, a drill, and something to sand the buttons smooth. Wood and antler are the easiest materials to work with, but don't discount bone, shell, and nut husks.

Antler tips are good for **oblong buttons**. Secure the antler in a vice and drill two holes through from the side. After the holes are drilled, saw off your button. Finish by sanding rough surfaces smooth. Stain if you want.

When the antler or stick is large enough in diameter for a **round or oval button,** drill holes in the center pithy part, and then cut buttons from the antler or stick. Rounding or beveling the edges of the buttonholes with a small, sharp rock will prevent the thread from being cut.

Buttons from bone and shell take a little more work because you are working with a flattened surface that needs to be rounded. Drill the holes before cutting out the button to prevent splitting. Grind the buttons round on a rock

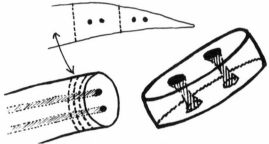

or concrete, or just pick ones that are already the shape you want. Many shells have natural holes and don't need drilling.

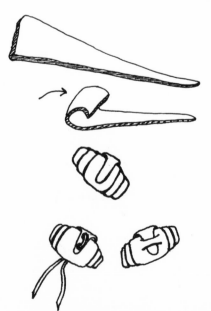

Making a **rolled-leather button** is really easy. Cut out a long thin triangle and roll it from the thick edge to the point. One way to finish the button is to punch two holes through the leather roll with a bone awl and lace a piece of leather through this hole; tie the loose ends of the lacing to the garment. Another way to finish up the roll button is to cut two slits in the wrap just before the triangular end and feed this triangular point through the slits like a belt buckle. Use the final point to sew the button onto the garment.

BOOT MOCCASINS

Now we are down to the feet. This boot moccasin pattern really joins old and new technologies. Duct tape and plastic make the pattern. You will need duct tape, a plastic bag or old sock you don't mind cutting up, scissors, a pen, a paper bag, leather, sinew or thread, and a glover's needle.

While you make the pattern, wear on your feet whatever you plan to wear in the finished boots. Then stick a plastic bag or old sock over the larger of your two feet (most folks have larger left feet), and **duct tape your entire foot** up to the height you want the boot to be. As you tape your foot, you *must* put your full weight down; otherwise, the pattern will be too small and the toes will bind.

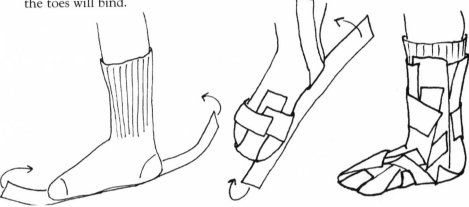

When you are all taped up, draw seams on the tape like this:

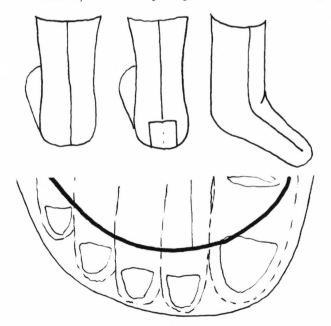

Draw the arching toe seam from the top of the pinky to the first knuckle on the big toe, following the curve along the bottom of your toenails.

Then cut along the drawn seams (front, back, and toe) to remove the pattern from your foot.

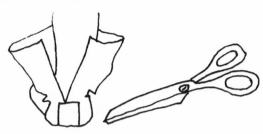

To make a final pattern, you need to transfer the tape pattern to paper and add the shaded elements shown in the drawing.

Snip the toe open to get it to lay flat and make the proper paper pattern. It is important to snip straight,

consistent cuts around the toe arc like the sun's rays. This way you get a true fit.

Spread the toe section and draw the toe outline on paper 1/8 inch above so you have material to pucker the toe. Add two flaps on the leg so you can close up the boot and keep out dirt.

Lay the paper pattern out on the leather and trace. Be sure to work on the inside so your marks don't show. Remember to turn the paper pattern over for the opposite foot!

When you have cut out two boots, cut a 7-foot, 1/2-inch-thick lacing for each boot.

String a needle and get ready to sew. Push the heel tab out of the way and sew the back seam from the bottom up.

Sew the heel tab in place.

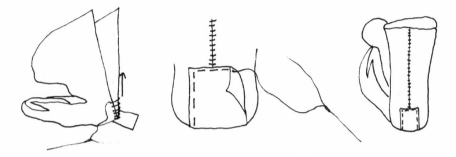

Sew the top middle seam from the toe end up toward the ankle.

As you get close to the ankle, try the boot on and end the seam at the point where you can just pull the boot on.

Now sew up the toe seam, puckering the toe material evenly as you sew for an attractive appearance and a good fit. Start at the center and work the puckers in on one side. Then return to center and work the other side. This gives more consistent puckers.

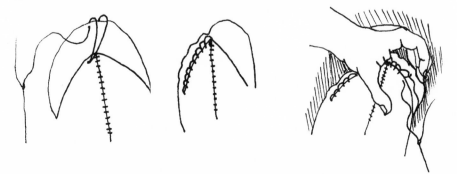

The last thing to do is to stitch the lacing to the heel tab.

You're finished! These boots are very stylish and comfortable. They are not as warm or waterproof as felted boots . . . but that's another book!

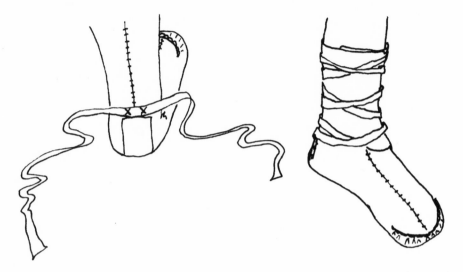

If you want more water resistance in your boots, rub rendered fat into the soles and sides of the boots. When the soles wear out, just sew on new ones!

You'll find clothes made from natural materials are easy to wear and so breathable they can be worn comfortably in a wide range of temperatures. The warmth and water repellency of fur is terrific. The suppleness of leather is unbeatable. There are many other animal and plant fibers that make useful and attractive attire. Have fun designing your wardrobe!